Warm Knits, Cool Gifts

to Leila and Ada

Published in the United States by Potter Craft, an imprint of the Crown Publishing Group,
a division of Random House, Inc., New York.
www.crownpublishing.com
www.pottercraft.com

POTTER CRAFT and colophon is a registered trademark of Random House, Inc.

Library of Congress Cataloging-in-Publication Data
Melville, Sally.
Warm knits, cool gifts : celebrate the love of knitting and family with more than 35 charming designs /
Sally Melville, Caddy Melville Ledbetter.
p. cm.
Includes bibliographical references and index.
ISBN 978-0-307-40873-0
1. Knitting—Patterns. I. Ledbetter, Caddy Melville. II. Title.
TT825.M4565 2010
746.43'2041—dc22   2010003103

Printed in China

Design by Rita Sowins / Sowins Design
Photography by Heather Weston

10 9 8 7 6 5 4 3 2 1

First Edition

Warm Knits, Cool Gifts

Celebrate the Love of Knitting & Family with More Than 35 Charming Designs

Sally Melville & Caddy Melville Ledbetter

POTTER CRAFT

New York

Contents

Introduction

This book came from an event, and here is its story.

I was walking through a farm in winter—watching families pick out their Christmas trees, take sleigh rides through the woods, wrap their hands around cups of hot chocolate, and throw snow at each other—when I realized that *winter* is my favorite season! I love the snow; I love the cold; I love the holidays!

And I love the knitting we do for this time of year: shawls to wrap up in, hats to pull over our ears, wool sweaters to keep us warm, heirloom pieces for the holidays, ornaments for the tree, and knitted gifts for those we love. So it didn't seem a far stretch to plan a book around these possibilities.

The chapter introductions speak to the particulars of knitting for babies and children, of making gifts for family and friends, of staying fashionable while keeping warm, and of preparing for the holidays. So I'll leave the particulars of these issues for later.

But here I'll say the obvious—that this book is my contribution to a long and wonderful tradition of knitting through the year in anticipation of and, yes, enjoyment of winter. I hope you use this book to honor that tradition by busying your hands, delighting your senses, and warming your heart.

In addition, and because I like to teach, there are lots of little teaching tips throughout the book—on the subjects of *inspiration, technique,* and *fit.* These tips answer questions I am often asked and will help you become a more informed, thoughtful, intuitive knitter. Even if you don't knit a particular pattern, you might want to look for them.

And, oh yes, it's a complete and absolute joy to again share this experience with my daughter! We continue to "work well together" and to make garments that conform to the concepts of our previous book, *Mother-Daughter Knits.* (All the sweater patterns indicate the style of the garment plus suggested lengths, based upon the principles of the "Knit to Flatter and Fit" chapter of our other book. See the Notes on Fit section, page 174, for a synopsis of this material.) —SALLY

for the
Wee Ones

It is one of knitting's longest and best-loved traditions that we knit
for the little ones in our lives. (And I am certainly inspired to do so for my
two new granddaughters!) But it's important that we knit
what babies and children want and/or can appreciate—by choosing
appropriately for style, color, and yarn.

During the first month of life, babies are most attracted to contrasting dark and light patterns, so a stationary black and white item will fascinate them. Within a few months, babies can track moving objects and see primary colors, so their eyes will follow the same black-and-white item or a red-yellow-blue piece on a moving mobile. Then in early childhood, the color cones in the eyes mature, and young children can distinguish (and might prefer) the secondary colors—orange, green, and purple. Next comes an appreciation of the tertiary colors (colors produced by combing a primary with a nearby secondary), until finally the color cones are fully mature and they can appreciate a full range of complex colors. So what does this mean when we knit for babies?

If it is something the baby will *look at*, it should be knit in black and white or in primary colors. If it is to be an heirloom piece—that we hope will be appreciated for generations—it may be made in more complex colors that adults will not tire of.

And what about knitting for the children in all those years between?

If it is something a child will want to *wear*, it should be in a style the child will think is "cool." (For reasons explained in the garment's story, I knew the hoodie, page 25, to be a safe and secure choice for this book. And the other garment that seemed an appropriate addition was the ubiquitous "sport" sweater, page 36.) And then when we knit these garments, we want to choose colors suitable for the age and preference of the child. (I chose classic, "cool" colors for the hoodie and bright, "team" colors for the sport sweater.)

See the introduction to the next chapter for an extension of the "knitting for children" discussion.

—SALLY

Blended Baby Blanket

DESIGNED BY SALLY

When we think "babies" we think "heirloom baby blanket." But that could mean lace-weight yarn and months of knitting over an intricate pattern. How could I make this a quickly-knit piece, accessible by not-very-experienced knitters? How could we have it all . . . something lovely, soft, easy, and very much to be treasured? The answer was to double the lace-weight yarn and let the colors flow!

Some might question the use of wool for a baby. But we need to remember that while some babies prefer soft and satiny surfaces, others prefer soft and fluffy. And this wool is very, very soft. Ada, Caddy's new baby, chose *this* blanket as her favorite—the one she needs to have close when going to sleep!

SKILL LEVEL
Intermediate

SIZE
All measurements are approximate.
Measurements (after washing) 37" x 37" (94cm x 94cm)

MATERIALS
> 470yd (425m) / 1 skein Malabrigo Lace (100% baby merino, each approximately 1¾oz [50g] and 470yd [425m]), (⓪) lace, in each of the following 6 colors:
> 19 (pollen), C1
> 72 (apricot), C2
> 17 (pink frost), C3
> 83 (water green), C4
> 37 (lettuce), C5
> 35 (frank ochre), C6
> One circular needle, size 9 (5.5mm), 20" (50cm) or longer
> 2 spare circular needles, size 9 (5.5mm) or smaller, any length
> *Optional* One crochet hook, size 7 (4.5mm)

GAUGE
Approximately 16 stitches and 32 rows (16 garter ridges) = 4" (10cm) in garter stitch and with yarn doubled
Gauge does not matter.

PATTERN NOTES
1. The yarn is doubled throughout. You could divide skeins in half (as you wind them into balls), or you could knit from the inside plus the outside of a wound ball.
2. On the schematic, heavy lines indicate where pieces are attached while working (so there are no seams). If you feel this makes the piece too challenging, you could knit these pieces without joining as you go. To do so, you will bind off the edges of the first, fourth, and sixth pieces, and you will sew these pieces together where shown by the heavy lines on the schematic.

Blanket

FIRST PIECE
With two strands of C1, crochet cast on 48 stitches.

✳ TECHNIQUE ✳
I used the crochet cast-on (see Glossary, page 167) because it mimics the bound-off edge. But if you prefer, you may work the long-tail cast-on and then only knit 15 rows.

***With two strands of C1, knit to 16 rows (8 garter ridges) from beginning.
Cut one strand of C1. Introduce one strand of C2.

✳ TECHNIQUE ✳

At all color changes, leave 8" (20.5cm) tails. Knit the first stitch of the row with two strands of the new color(s), then pick up the tails and knit them in (see Glossary, page 167) over the first 5–6 stitches of this row—4" (10cm) remain of the tails. With a tapestry needle, sew in the remaining tails when finishing.

With C1 plus C2, knit 16 rows (8 garter ridges).
Cut C1. Introduce a second strand of C2.
With two strands of C2, knit 16 rows.
Cut one strand of C2. Introduce one strand of C3.
With C2 plus C3, knit 16 rows.
Cut C2. Introduce a second strand of C3.
With two strands of C3, knit 16 rows.
Cut one strand of C3. Introduce one strand of C4.***
With C3 plus C4, knit 16 rows.
Cut C3 and C4.
Put stitches onto spare needle.

SECOND PIECE

✳ TECHNIQUE ✳

1. When you pick up along an edge (see Glossary, page 167), slip the needle through the garter ridges close to, but not right at, the edge. Make sure to slip your needle through the same part of every ridge each time.

2. For most pieces, it does not matter which direction you slip your needle when picking up: if it matters, the pattern will tell you so. But when you begin working, always begin with a right-side row.

With RS facing, and including the cast-on edge of the First Piece, slip main needle through 48 ridges along right edge of First Piece—48 stitches on needle.
For all following pieces, if you get 49 stitches when including a cast-on or bound-off edge, eliminate the extra stitch by working k2tog at the beginning or end of the next row.
*With two strands of C4, knit 16 rows.
Cut one strand of C4. Introduce one strand of C5.
With C4 plus C5, knit 16 rows.
Cut C4. Introduce a second strand of C5.
With two strands of C5, knit 16 rows.
Cut one strand of C5. Introduce one strand of C6.
With C5 plus C6, knit 16 rows.
Cut C5. Introduce a second strand of C6.
With two strands of C6, knit 16 rows.
Cut one strand of C6. Introduce one strand of C1.
With C1 plus C6, knit 14 rows.*
Bind off loosely.

THIRD PIECE

With RS facing, and including the cast-on edge of the First Piece, slip main needle through 48 ridges along left edge of First Piece—48 stitches on needle.
****With one strand of C1 plus one strand of C6, knit 16 rows.
Cut C1. Introduce a second strand of C6.
With two strands of C6, knit 16 rows.
Cut one strand of C6. Introduce one strand of C5.
With C6 plus C5, knit 16 rows.
Cut C6. Introduce a second strand of C5.
With two strands of C5, knit 16 rows.
Cut one strand of C5. Introduce one strand of C4.
With C5 plus C4, knit 16 rows.
Cut C5. Introduce a second strand of C4.
With two strands of C4, knit 14 rows.
Bind off loosely.

FOURTH PIECE

With RS facing, and including bound-off edge of Second Piece, slip main needle through 48 ridges along top edge of Second Piece—48 stitches on needle.
**With one strand of C4 and one strand of C3, knit to 16 rows.
Cut C4. Introduce a second strand of C3.
With two strands of C3, knit 16 rows.
Cut one strand of C3. Introduce one strand of C2.
With C3 plus C2, knit 16 rows.
Cut C3. Introduce a second strand of C2.
With two strands of C2, knit 16 rows.
Cut one strand of C2. Introduce one strand of C1.
With C2 plus C1, knit 16 rows.
Cut C2. Introduce a second strand of C1.
With two strands of C1, knit 16 rows.
Put stitches onto spare needle.

FIFTH PIECE

With RS facing, slip main needle, from left to right, through 48 stitches of First Piece (from spare needle) and then through 48 ridges along left edge of Fourth Piece—end at top of Fourth Piece, 96 stitches on needle.
Work color pattern from * to * as Second Piece, AT THE SAME TIME joining Fifth Piece to First Piece by working all rows as follows.
RS Rows K47, then k2tog (knitting last stitch of Fifth Piece together with next stitch of First Piece). Turn.
WS Rows K48.
End with 16 rows of C1 plus C6—0 stitches remain from First Piece.
Leave stitches on main needle.

SIXTH PIECE

With RS facing, slide stitches of Fifth Piece to other end of main needle. Bring free end of main needle around to bound-off edge of Third Piece and, including bound-off edge, slip needle through 48 ridges along top edge of Third Piece—48 stitches on left needle, 48 stitches on (what now becomes) right needle.

The needle points will be at the intersection of the Fifth and Third Pieces.

Do not weave in the tails after introducing C3 and C4: use these tails to close the small hole that forms at the corner.

With one strand of C3 and one strand of C4, knit 2 rows over 48 stitches at top of Third Piece—48 stitches from Fifth Piece remain on right needle.

Continue with color pattern from ** to end as Fourth Piece, AT THE SAME TIME working all following RS rows as follows (to join Sixth Piece to Fifth Piece).

RS Rows K1 (of Sixth Piece), pass last stitch of Fifth Piece over stitch just knit, then k47.

WS Rows K48. Turn.

End with 16 rows of two strands of C1—0 stitches remain from Fifth Piece.

Put stitches onto spare needle.

SEVENTH PIECE

With RS facing, slip main needle through 48 ridges along top edge of Fifth Piece—48 stitches on needle. Work color pattern from *** to *** as First Piece.

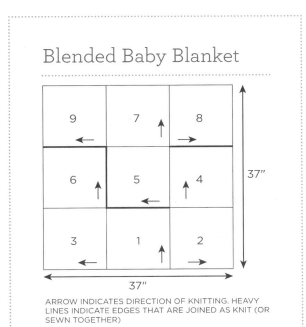

Blended Baby Blanket

37"

37"

ARROW INDICATES DIRECTION OF KNITTING. HEAVY LINES INDICATE EDGES THAT ARE JOINED AS KNIT (OR SEWN TOGETHER)

With C3 plus C4, knit 14 rows.
Bind off loosely.

EIGHTH PIECE

With RS facing, and including bound-off edge of Seventh Piece, slip main needle through 48 ridges along right edge of Seventh Piece so point ends at beginning of Seventh Piece. Slip other end of this needle from right to left through 48 stitches from spare needle at top of Fourth Piece—48 stitches on right needle, 48 stitches on left needle.

The needle points will be at the intersection of the Fourth and Seventh Pieces.

Do not weave in the tails after introducing two strands of C4: use these tails to close the small hole that forms at the corner.

With two strands of C4, knit 2 rows over 48 stitches at side of Seventh Piece—48 stitches from Fourth Piece remain on right needle.

Continue with color pattern from * to end as Second Piece, AT THE SAME TIME working all following RS rows as follows (to join Eighth Piece to Fourth Piece).

RS Rows K1 (of Eighth Piece), pass last stitch of Fourth Piece over stitch just knit, then k47.

WS Rows K48. Turn.

End with 14 rows of C6 plus C1.

Final Row K1, pass the stitch of Fourth Piece over stitch just knit, then bind off loosely—0 stitches remain from Fourth Piece.

NINTH PIECE

With RS facing, and including bound-off edge of Seventh Piece, slip main needle through 48 stitches from spare needle at top edge of Sixth Piece and 48 ridges along left edge of Seventh Piece—end at top of Seventh Piece, 96 stitches on needle.

Work color pattern from **** to end as Third Piece, AT THE SAME TIME joining Ninth Piece to Sixth Piece by working all rows as follows.

RS Rows K47, then k2tog (knitting last stitch of Ninth Piece together with next stitch of Sixth Piece). Turn.

WS Rows K48.

End with 14 rows of two strands of C4.

Final Row Bind off loosely, ending with k2tog— 0 stitches remain from Sixth Piece.

FINISHING

Sew in all remaining tails, closing any holes at corners. To block, wash as directed by a wool-wash solution. Lay flat to dry.

Heirloom Jumper

DESIGNED BY CADDY

I was asked by the publishers to make a bunting bag. But I was curious of their color choice. A beige bunting bag? Now I know how my mom felt all those times I had asked her to knit me something really plain. But as I finished the garment, I have to say the beige kind of grew on me. The texture of the stitch pattern looks wonderful worked in a neutral, and I can really see this piece being the kind of thing that could be passed from generation to generation without ever looking dated. But as I worked through the design and made legs and arms—for modern babies and their car seats—it became more of a "jumper."

SKILL LEVEL
Intermediate

SIZES
> 0–3 months
> Finished chest circumference 19″ (48.5cm)
> Finished length (from shoulder to ankle, relaxed) 19″ (48.5cm)
> Finished length (underarm to inseam) 10½″ (26.5cm)
> Finished sleeve length 11½″ (29cm)

MATERIALS
> 380yd [345m] / 6 skeins Berroco Touche (50% cotton, 50% rayon, each approximately 1¾oz [50g] and 89yd [82m]), in color 7944 (pebble), ③ light
> Two size 6 (4mm) circular needles, or size needed to obtain gauge, 20″ (51cm)
> One set of 5 dpns, size 6 (4mm), or size needed to obtain gauge
> One stitch marker
> One stitch holder
> 6 buttons, ½″ (13mm) wide

GAUGE
22 stitches and 30 rows = 4″ (10cm) in stitch pattern

PATTERN NOTE
The buttonhole band does not have actual buttonholes because buttons are easily forced through the ribbed edge.

STITCH PATTERN
(over a multiple of 10 stitches)
Row or Round 1 *P4, k1, p1, k4; repeat from * to end.
Row or Round 2 *P3, k2, p2, k3; repeat from * to end.
Row or Round 3 *P2, k2, p1, k1, p2, k2; repeat from * to end.
Row or Round 4 *P1, k2, p2, k2, p2, k1; repeat from * to end.
Row or Round 5 *K2, p3, k3, p2; repeat from * to end.
Row or Round 6 *K1, p4, k4, p1; repeat from * to end.

✳ TECHNIQUE ✳
1. When working in the round, all rows of chart are RS rows; read all rows from right to left.
2. When working back and forth, read all RS rows of chart from right to left and all WS rows from left to right.
3. If working from written pattern, the rows are symmetrical so are worked the same whether a RS or WS row.

✳ FLATTER & FIT ✳
Sleeve length is measured from center body to end of sleeve. For more information, see Glossary, page 167.

Jumper

LOWER BODY PIECE

RIGHT LEG

Long-tail cast on 40 stitches.

Distribute stitches evenly over 4 dpns—10 on each needle.

Join to work in the round, being careful not to twist cast-on edge. Place marker at beginning of round.

Purl 2 rounds.

Beginning with round 1, work chart until piece measures 5" (12.5cm). End at marker.

(Shorten or lengthen for leg length here.)

Cut yarn.

Note what stitch pattern round you ended with.

Put all stitches onto holder.

LEFT LEG

Work as Right Leg, ending with same round. Do not cut yarn.

LOWER BODY AND BUTTONHOLE BAND

Return to Left Leg stitches (on holder).

Next Row (RS)

- Count 20 stitches back from the last stitch of the Left Leg
- Slip those 20 stitches (the front of the Left Leg) onto one circular needle (you are now at the yarn)
- Turn, and e-wrap cast on 10 stitches onto the circular needle (for the front of the crotch)
- Turn, and starting at the tail of the Right Leg, work next row of stitch pattern over 20 stitches (the front of the Right Leg)
- Continuing with the same row of stitch pattern, work the remaining 20 stitches from the Right Leg onto a second circular needle (the back of the Right Leg)
- Turn and e-wrap cast on 10 stitches (for the back of the crotch)
- Turn, and continuing with the same row of stitch pattern, work 20 stitches from the Left Leg (the back of the Left Leg)
- Continue with the same row of the stitch pattern over 20 stitches (the front of the Left Leg), then over 10 stitches (the front of the crotch)—to the beginning of the Right Leg
- Turn (so WS is facing).

There will be 100 stitches on your needle.

You are using circular needles but will not be working in the round.

FRONT EDGING

Next Row (WS) E-wrap cast on 5 stitches, p1, k1, p1, k1, p1, work stitch pattern to end.

These 5 stitches are the buttonhole band. As soon as it is comfortable, use only one circular needle.

Continue in stitch pattern as established—with 5 1x1 rib stitches at the end of RS rows and at the beginning of WS rows—until piece measures 10½" (26.5cm) above crotch. End after working row 6.

Bind off in pattern.

LEFT SLEEVE AND UPPER BODY

With circular needle, long-tail cast on 30 stitches.

Knit 1 (WS) row.

Beginning with row 1 of stitch pattern, work 8 rows from chart. End after working row 2.

*Increase Row (RS) Kf&b, work stitch pattern as established to last stitch, kf&b.

Next 9 Rows Work center 30 stitches in stitch pattern as established; work increased stitch(es) in stockinette stitch.

Repeat from * 4 times more—40 stitches.

Work even until piece measures 9" (23cm). End after working a WS row.

(Shorten or lengthen for sleeve length here.)

Work 20 stitches, then put these 20 stitches onto a holder (for Left Back). Do not cut yarn.

LEFT FRONT

Work chart over remaining 20 stitches as follows.

RS Rows Beginning at center of chart, work 5 stitches; work chart over next 10 stitches; end with k5.

WS Rows P5; work chart as established over 15 stitches.

Work until Left Front (neck opening) measures 2½" (6.5cm). End after working a WS row.

BUTTONHOLE BAND

Work 1x1 rib for 4 rows, then bind off in rib.

LEFT BACK

Return to stitches on holder with WS facing.
Work next row of chart over these 20 stitches as follows.
WS Rows Beginning at center of chart, work 5 stitches; work chart over next 10 stitches; end with P5.
RS Rows K5; work chart as established over 15 stitches.
Work until neck opening measures 2½" (6.5cm).
Bind off in pattern.

RIGHT SLEEVE AND UPPER BODY

Work as Left Sleeve and Upper Body but without Buttonhole Band.
Bind off in pattern after neck opening measures 2½" (6.5cm).

FINISHING

Match front edge of Right Upper Body to right front edge of Lower Body.
Sew Right Upper Body to 25 bound-off stitches of Lower Body.
Sew Right Sleeve seam.
Match edges of buttonhole bands (of Left Upper and Lower Body pieces).
Sew buttonhole band of Upper Body to buttonhole band of Lower Body, then sew Left Upper Body to 25 bound-off stitches of Lower Body.
Sew Left Sleeve seam.

Sew Right and Left Upper Body bound-off edges together at center back.
Sew back of Upper Body pieces to bound-off stitches of Lower Body across back.

✳ TECHNIQUE ✳

For a newborn, you could use a contrasting yarn to sew the legs together at the foot end. Then, as the baby grows taller and wears socks, you can undo these seams.

HOOD

Beginning at Right Front neck edge, and with RS facing, pick up and knit 2 stitches for every 3 rows across Right Front, across Back neck, across Left Front, and across buttonhole band.
Next Row Count stitches: purl this row, increasing or decreasing as needed for a multiple of 10 + 2 stitches.
All Rows Sl 1 purlwise, work stitch pattern to last stitch, k1.
Work until hood measures 7½" (19cm). Bind off in pattern.
Fold hood in half and sew bound-off edges together.

Sew 6 buttons evenly along Right Front edge, with top button 1½" (3.8cm) from beginning of hood and lower button ½" (13mm) from crotch.
Force buttons through buttonhole band to create buttonholes.

Heirloom Jumper

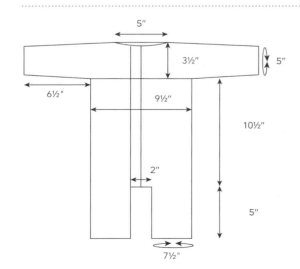

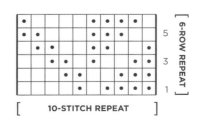

knit on RS, purl on WS

• purl on RS, knit on WS

Ear Flap Baby Hat

DESIGNED BY CADDY

As I write this, I am three weeks from giving birth to my first child . . . and all I have knit for this baby is a hat that took about two hours to make. I had so many good intentions of completely decking out my baby in hand-knits, but nine months just isn't as long as you might think! But if all my baby gets on arrival to the world is a hat, at least it's a really, really cute one. Maybe I should embroider it with "I spent nine months in the womb and all I got was this hat."

SKILL LEVEL
Easy

SIZE

> 0–6 months
> Finished circumference 13″ (33cm)
> Finished circumference, stretched 19″ (48.5cm)
> Finished height 6″ (15cm)

MATERIALS

> 75yd (68m) / 1 skein Jil Eaton Minnow Merino (100% extra fine merino, each approximately 1¾ oz [50g] and 77yd [70m]), in color 4750 (yellow), (5) bulky
> One set of 5 dpns, size 10 (6mm), or size needed to obtain gauge
> One crochet hook, size 8 (5mm) or larger
> Stitch marker

GAUGE
14 stitches and 24 rows = 4″ (10cm) in stitch pattern

Hat

Long-tail cast on 48 stitches.
Distribute stitches evenly over 4 dpns—12 stitches on each needle.
Join to work in the round, being careful not to twist cast-on edge. Place marker at beginning of round.
Purl 4 rounds, then knit 4 rounds.
Repeat the last 8 rounds 4 times more.
Decrease Round Knit to last 2 stitches on each needle, k2tog.

Repeat Decrease Round 9 times more—2 stitches on each needle. Cut yarn.
Thread tapestry needle through remaining stitches, remove needles, and pull taut.

FINISHING
EAR FLAPS (MAKE 2)
With RS facing, and beginning anywhere along cast-on edge, pick up and knit 10 stitches.

✳ TECHNIQUE ✳

When picking up and knitting along an edge (see Glossary, page 167), you will not get holes if you always insert your needle into spaces so that you then see two threads on your needle.

✳ FLATTER & FIT ✳

This hat will look small when done, but it really will stretch to fit a child up to at least 6 months of age. Go to www.sallymelvilleknits.com and click on "Books" to see how to make this hat for an adult.

Ear Flap Baby Hat

6"

13"

*Knit 6 rows.

Decrease Row K1, ssk, knit to last 3 stitches, k2tog, k1.

Knit 4 rows.

Repeat Decrease Row.

Knit 2 rows.

Repeat Decrease Row once—4 stitches.

Next Row Ssk, k2tog.

Bind off.

With RS facing, and beginning 3" (7.5cm) along cast-on edge from end of first flap, pick up and knit 10 stitches.

Work a second Ear Flap as from * to end of first flap.

TASSELS (MAKE 2)

Cut three lengths of yarn 9" (23cm) long.

Fold all three in half and, with a crochet hook, pull fold through tip of ear flap—to form loop on crochet hook. Draw tails through loop. Halfway down the tails, make an overhand knot. Trim tails to suit.

Baby Overalls

DESIGNED BY CADDY

Every baby needs a pair of overalls: it's an unwritten rule. These were first made in yellow and orange and for a little girl named Chicken—actually, her name's Ayan, but everyone calls her Chicken or The Chick. (She has, all on her own, started correcting people and informing them of her real name, and she's only a year-and-a-half.) I still call her Chicken, and I always will, but I hope she will forgive me one day for dressing the girl named Chicken in yellow and orange overalls.

SKILL LEVEL
Intermediate

SIZES
> 3–6 months (6–9 months, 9–12 months)
> Finished chest 24 (26½, 29½)" (61 [67, 74.5]cm)
> Finished length (from top of bib to ankle) 20¼ (22, 23¾)" (51.5 [56, 60.5]cm)
> Finished length (from top of bib to inseam) 13½ (14¾, 16)" (34.5 [37.5, 40.5]cm)
Model was made in size 3–6 months.

MATERIALS
> Louet MerLin (70% merino wool, 30% linen, each approximately 3½ oz [100g] and 156yd [142m]), **4** medium, in the following amounts and colors:
> 240 (280, 325)yd (216 [252, 293]m) / 2 (2, 3) skeins, in color 18 (aqua) MC
> 140 (162, 190)yd (126 [146, 171]m / 1 (2, 2) skeins, in color 36 (linen grey) CC
> One pair size 8 (5mm) needles, or size needed to obtain gauge
> Stitch holder
> 7 buttons, ¾" (2cm) wide
> *Optional* 2 more buttons, ¾" (2cm) wide

GAUGE
18 stitches and 24 rows = 4" (10cm) in stockinette stitch

PATTERN NOTES
1. Separate CC into 2 balls if you don't have 2 balls already.
2. There is no need for buttonholes; the stitch pattern allows enough stretch for buttons to fit through.
3. You will work the back and front upside down.

Overalls

BACK
BODY
With MC, long-tail cast on 38 (44, 50) stitches.

> ✳ FLATTER & FIT ✳
>
> My friends—and the yarn's label—assure me the overalls knit in this yarn can be safely machine washed and dried without a change in fit or size. But if you substitute yarns, do make sure the same is true of whatever you use.

Knit 5 rows.

Next Row (RS) With CC e-wrap cast on 8 stitches; with CC k12; with MC knit to end—46 (52, 58) stitches.

Next Row (WS) With CC e-wrap cast on 8 stitches; with CC p12; with MC p30 (36, 42); with CC p12—54 (60, 66) stitches.

✳ TECHNIQUE ✳

You are working intarsia (see Glossary, page 167), so cross yarns on wrong side at all color changes by always taking the color you have finished with over the color you are working next.

Next Row (RS) With CC k12, with MC k30 (36, 42), with CC k12.

Next Row (WS) With CC p12, with MC p30 (36, 42), with CC p12.

Repeat the last 2 rows until piece measures 8½ (9¼, 10)" (21.5 [23.5, 25.5]cm) from CC cast-on edges. End after working a WS row.

(Shorten or lengthen for finished body length here.)

RIGHT LEG

Continue with color changes as established.

Next Row (RS) K25 (27, 29), put these stitches on holder for Left Leg, bind off center 4 (6, 8) stitches, k25 (27, 29).

Beginning with a WS row, work even over 25 (27, 29) stitches of Right Leg until it measures 5½ (6, 6½)" (14 [15, 16.5]cm). End after working a RS row.

(Shorten or lengthen for finished leg length here.)

*Cut MC.

Next Row (WS) Purl in CC.

Next Row (RS) Purl in CC.

Next Row (WS) Knit in CC.

Repeat the last 2 rows twice more, then bind off.

LEFT LEG

Continue with color changes as established.

Return to stitches on holder, ready to work a WS row.

Beginning with a WS row, work even over 25 (27, 29) stitches of Left Leg until it measures same length as Right Leg. End after working a WS row.

**Cut MC.

Next Row (RS) Knit in CC.

Next Row (WS) Knit in CC.

Next Row (RS) Purl in CC.

Repeat the last 2 rows twice more, then bind off.

✳ FLATTER & FIT ✳

Babies grow faster in length than in girth, and knitting is stretchy, so if you want this to fit an older baby, knit more length where indicated, especially in the legs.

FRONT

BIB

With MC, long-tail cast on 32 (38, 44) stitches.
Knit 5 rows.

Next Row (RS) With CC k4, with MC k24 (30, 36), with CC k4.

Continuing in stockinette stitch, work even for 5 (7, 9) rows. End after working a WS row.

Increase Row (RS) With CC k4, with MC increase 1 in next stitch, knit to last 5 stitches, increase 1 in next stitch, with CC k4.

✳ TECHNIQUE ✳

Work all increases as lifted increases (see Glossary, page 167). These are the best increases in stockinette stitch.

Work 5 rows even.
Repeat the last 6 rows twice more—38 (44, 50) stitches.
Work even—in stockinette stitch and with color changes as established—until piece measures 5 (5½, 6)" (12.5 [14, 15]cm) . End after working a WS row.

BODY

Next Row (RS) With CC e-wrap cast on 8 stitches, with CC k12, with MC k30 (36, 42), with CC k4—46 (50, 56) stitches.

Next Row (WS) With CC e-wrap cast on 8 stitches, with CC p12, with MC p30 (36, 42) , with CC p12—54 (58, 66) stitches.

Work even to same length as Back from underarm to crotch. End after working a RS row.

Next Row (WS) P25 (27, 29), k4 (6, 8), p25 (27, 29).

LEFT LEG

Continue with color changes as established.

Next Row (RS) K25 (27, 29) stitches and put on holder for Right Leg. Bind off center 4 (6, 8) stitches, k25 (27, 29).

Next Row (WS) Purl to last 3 stitches, k3.

Next Row (RS) Knit.

Repeat the last 2 rows until Left Leg measures same length as Back Legs. End after working a RS row.

Work as Back Right Leg from * to end.

RIGHT LEG

Continue with color changes as established.

Return to stitches on holder, ready to work a WS row.

Next Row (WS) K3, purl to end.

Next Row (RS) Knit.

Repeat the last 2 rows until Right Leg measures same as Left Leg. End after working a WS row.

Work as Back Left Leg from ** to end.

Baby Overalls

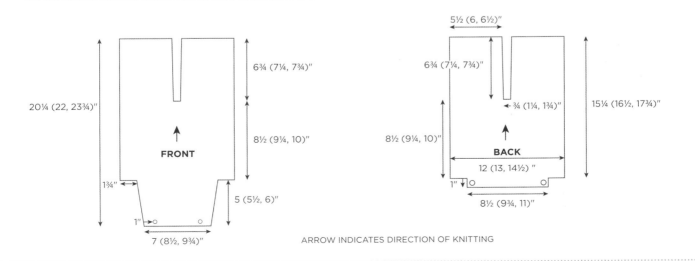

ARROW INDICATES DIRECTION OF KNITTING

FINISHING

UPPER BACK

With RS facing and MC, pick up and knit 1 stitch for every stitch across cast-on edge of Back—38 (44, 50) stitches.

✳ TECHNIQUE ✳

When picking up and knitting along an edge (see Glossary, page 67), you will not get holes if you always insert your needle into spaces so that you then see two threads on your needle.

Knit 1 row.
Decrease Row (RS) K1, ssk, knit to last 3 stitches, k2tog, k1.
Repeat the last 2 rows 10 (11, 12) times more—16 (20, 24) stitches.
Knit 1 row.

LEFT STRAP

Next Row (RS) K8 (10, 12). Put these stitches on holder for Right Strap. K8 remaining stitches.
Knit all rows until 8 stitches of Strap measure 4 (4½, 5)" (10 [11.5, 12.5]cm), then bind off.

RIGHT STRAP

Return to stitches on holder, ready to work a WS row.
Work as Left Strap from *** to ***.
Sew side seams.

INSEAM BUTTON BAND

With RS facing, MC, and beginning at cuff edge of Back Left Leg, pick up and knit 1 stitch for every 2 rows and 1 stitch for every stitch along entire inseam—approximately 45 (47, 53) stitches.
Knit 8 (9, 10) rows, then bind off.
Sew 5 buttons evenly spaced onto button band, placing middle button at center of crotch.

Sew 2 buttons to places marked by circles on schematic for Front.
Force buttons through garter stitch edge of Front Legs and Straps to create buttonholes.
Optional Sew 2 buttons to places marked by circles on schematic for Back.
Fold Fronts toward Back to reach these buttons, and push buttons through all layers.
This will tighten the overalls at the top of the side seams, which may be needed for some sizes.

Vested Hoodie

DESIGNED BY SALLY

Whenever I ask about designs for a book, a child or young adult usually responds with some version of "a hoodie, please." So here's a kid's hoodie—made to look like what I saw all the ever-so-cool young folk wearing at a ski hill . . . a vest over a hoodie. But I've found that there's no need to *actually* knit both pieces: here they are combined as one.

SKILL LEVEL
Intermediate

SIZES
> Child's 2–4 (6–8, 10–12)
> Finished chest 28 (32, 36)" (71 [81.5, 91.5]cm)
> Finished length 14 (17, 21)" (35.5 [43, 53.5]cm)
> Finished sleeve length 18 (22, 26)" (45.5 [56, 66]cm)
Model is shown in size 6–8.

MATERIALS
for Vest
> 170 (235, 325)yd (153 [210, 292]m) / 3 (4, 5) balls Plymouth Alpaca Boucle (90% alpaca, 10% nylon, each approximately 1¾ oz [50g] and 65yd [58m]), in color 14 (rust) A, (5) bulky

for Trim, Sleeves, Hood
> 335 (460, 635)yd (300 [415, 575]m) / 4 (5, 6) balls Cleckheaton Country Naturals 8-ply (85% wool, 10% acrylic, 5% viscose, each approximately 1¾ oz [50g] and 105yd [95m]), in color 1832 (gray) B, (4) medium
> One pair size 10 (6mm) needles, or size needed to obtain gauge
> One circular needle, size 6 (4mm), or size needed to obtain gauge, 20" (51cm)
> One circular needle, size 5 (3.75mm), 20" (51cm)
> 2 stitch holders
> 2 spare needles

✳ FLATTER & FIT ✳

You want to knit the size the child will wear, so always check fit against a garment that the child already wears. And remember that children are as various in height as adults, so after choosing the correct size—according to girth—be sure to knit the garment, and sleeves, to an appropriate length for the recipient. The pattern tells you where and when to adjust for this.

GAUGE
> 12 stitches and 22 rows = 4" (10cm) in stockinette stitch, with heavier yarn and over larger needles
> 20 stitches and 26 rows = 4" (10cm) in stockinette stitch, with lighter yarn and over middle-sized needles

Hoodie

VEST BACK

EDGING

With smallest needle and B, long-tail cast on 71 (81, 91) stitches.

Beginning with a purl row, work 4 rows in reverse stockinette (RSS). End after working a knit row. Cut B.
The purl (RSS) side of the edging and of the vest both become the RS of the garment.

BODY

Decrease Row With largest needles and A, *k1, skp, skp; repeat from * to last stitch, k1—43 (49, 55) stitches.

Beginning with a WS (knit) row, work RSS until piece measures 8 (9½, 12)" (20.5 [24, 30.5]cm). End after working a purl row.
The RSS side of the both the edging and the Vest is the right side of the garment.

(Shorten or lengthen for finished length here.)

SHAPE ARMHOLE

Bind off 2 (2, 3) stitches at beginning of next 2 rows—39 (45, 49) stitches.

Decrease Row (WS) K1, skp, knit to last 3 stitches, k2tog, k1.
Purl 1 row.

Repeat the last 2 rows 3 (4, 4) times more—31 (35, 39) stitches.

Work even until piece measures 13 (16, 20)" (33 [40.5, 51]cm). End after working a purl row.

SHAPE LEFT SHOULDER AND BACK NECK

Bind off 3 (3, 4) stitches at beginning of next row, work to 6 (8, 8) stitches on right needle. Put center 13 (13, 15) stitches onto holder for Back neck. Turn.
*Bind off 1 stitch at neck edge, work to end.

Bind off 2 (3, 3) stitches at armhole edge, work to end. Repeat from * once.

SHAPE RIGHT SHOULDER

Return to remaining 9 (11, 12) stitches, knit side facing. Knit 1 row.
Bind off 3 (3, 4) stitches at armhole edge, purl to end. Work as Shape Left Shoulder and Back Neck from * to end.

VEST FRONT

Work as Vest Back to 1" (2.5cm) above edging. End after working a knit row.

ESTABLISH POCKET STITCHES

Next Row P9 (12, 15), *yo, p1; repeat from * to last 9 (12, 15) stitches, yo, p9 (12, 15).

POCKET LINING

Next Row K9 (12, 15), put first yo and next stitch onto spare needle and on purl side of work, *knit next yo to twist it, put next stitch onto spare needle and on purl side of work; repeat from * to stitch before last yo, put last stitch and last yo onto spare needle on purl side of work, k9 (12, 15)—42 (48, 54) stitches on needle, 27 stitches on spare needle on purl side.

Increase Row Purl, increasing 1 stitch in center of row—43 (49, 55) stitches.

Continue RSS over 43 (49, 55) stitches (stitches of Vest plus pocket lining) until lining measures 5 (5½, 6)" (12.5 [14, 15.5]cm). End after working a knit row. Put 43 (49, 55) stitches onto second spare needle.

POCKET FRONT

Next Row Return to 27 stitches on first spare needle, purl side facing.

With largest needles and A, purl yo to twist it, p25, purl yo to twist it.

Work RSS over 27 stitches to 1" (2.5cm). End after working a purl row.

Decrease Row (WS) K1, skp, knit to last 3 stitches, k2tog, k1—25 pocket stitches.

Repeat Decrease Row when pocket front measures 2½" (6.5cm)—23 pocket stitches.

Repeat Decrease Row when pocket front measures 4"
(10cm)—21 pocket stitches.
Continue RSS over 21 stitches until pocket front is
same length as pocket lining. End after working a knit
row. Cut A. Put these stitches onto spare needle.

JOIN POCKET LINING AND POCKET FRONT
Return to 43 (49, 55) stitches, purl side facing.
Next Row P11 (14, 17) from back needle, p2tog across
the next 21 stitches of both spare needles (working
the stitches from pocket front together with pocket
lining), p11 (14, 17) from back needle—43 (49, 55)
stitches.
Continue in RSS until piece measures same length as
Back to armhole. End after working a purl row.

SHAPE ARMHOLE
Work as Vest Back, Shape Armhole—31 (35, 39) stitches.
Work even until piece measures 11 (14, 18)" (28 [35.5,
45.5]cm). End after working a purl row.

SHAPE RIGHT FRONT NECK AND SHOULDER
Next Row K12 (14, 15). Put center 7 (7, 9) stitches onto
second holder for Front neck. Turn.
*Continuing in RSS as established, shape neck as
follows.
Bind off 2 stitches at next neck edge, work to end.
Bind off 1 stitch at next 3 neck edges, work to end.
AT THE SAME TIME, when armhole measures same
length as Back, shape shoulder by binding off at
armhole edge 3 (3, 4) stitches once, then 2 (3, 3)
stitches twice.

SHAPE LEFT FRONT NECK AND SHOULDER
Return to remaining 12 (14, 15) stitches, knit side facing.
Work 2 rows even.
Work as Shape Right Front Neck and Shoulder from *
to end.

SLEEVES
EDGING
With smallest needle and B, cast on 34 (36, 40)
stitches.
Beginning with a purl row, work 4 rows in RSS. End
after working a knit row.

BODY
Change to middle-sized needle. Beginning with a knit
row, work 6 (6, 8) rows in stockinette stitch.
Increase Row (RS) K1, work lifted increase in next stitch,
knit to last 2 stitches, work lifted increase in next stitch, k1.

✳ TECHNIQUE ✳
Lifted increases (see Glossary, page 167) are the best
increases in stockinette stitch.

Work 5 (5, 7) rows even.
Repeat the last 6 (6, 8) rows 6 (9, 14) times more—48
(56, 70) stitches.
Work even until Sleeve measures 9 (12½, 15½)"
(23 [32, 39.5]cm). End after working a purl row.
(Shorten or lengthen for sleeve length here.)

CAP
Bind off 3 (4, 6) stitches at beginning of next 2
rows—42 (48, 58) stitches.
Decrease Row K1, skp, knit to last 3 stitches, k2tog, k1.
Purl 1 row.
Repeat the last 2 rows 10 (13, 18) times more—20
stitches.
Bind off 2 stitches at beginning of next 2 rows.
Bind off remaining 16 stitches.

FINISHING
ARMHOLE EDGING
Sew shoulder seams.
With smallest needle and B, and with purl side facing,
pick up and knit 3 (4, 6) stitches at armhole bind-offs
and 1 stitch for every row around armhole edge—
approximately 50 (66, 84) stitches.

✳ TECHNIQUE ✳
I don't normally like to suggest a total of stitches after
picking up for armholes because your row gauge
might not match mine. But since the bouclee yarn is
difficult to read I want to give you an approximate
number of stitches. The same is true for the pocket
edging.

Work 4 rows in RSS, beginning with a knit (WS) row
and ending with a purl row. Bind off knitwise.

NECK EDGING
With smallest needle and B, and with purl side of
garment facing, begin at left shoulder seam to pick up
and knit as follows:
- 16 stitches between shoulder seams and stitches
  on holder for Front neck
- [k1, work lifted increase in next stitch] 3 (3, 4)
  times, then end with k1 across stitches on holder
  for Front neck—10 (10, 13) stitches
- [k1, work lifted increase in next stitch] 6 (6, 7)

times, then k1 across stitches on holder for Back neck—19 (19, 22) stitches

- 7 stitches between shoulder seams and stitches on holder for Back neck

—approximately 75 (75, 81) stitches.

Turn (so knit side of garment is facing), and work in rounds as follows.

Next Round Knit, increasing evenly to 78 (78, 86) stitches.

Next 4 Rounds Knit.

Turn (so purl side of garment is facing).

Next Round Knit. Cut yarn, leaving long tail to sew down edging.

HOOD

Slip stitches onto left needle until points of circular needle are at center Front.

Change to middle-sized needle. Working back and forth, work stockinette stitch to 1″ (2.5cm). End after working a purl row.

Increase Row (RS) Knit to right shoulder seam, *k4, increase 1 in next stitch; repeat from * 6 times more—85 (85, 93) stitches.

Continue in stockinette stitch until hood measures 11 (12, 13)″ (28 [30.5, 33]cm).

Fold hood in half, right sides together, and use smallest needle to 3-needle bind-off two halves together.

Use tail from neck edging to sew neck edging down to its selvedge.

Be careful to sew the edging down loosely enough that the head can still pass through.

HOOD EDGING

Return to center Front.

With smallest needle and B, and with RS of hood facing, pick up and knit 3 stitches for every 4 rows around entire hood edge.

Working back and forth, work 5 rows in RSS, beginning and ending with a knit (WS) row.

Bind off purlwise, leaving long tail.

With tail, sew hood edging to its selvedge, sewing edging closed and to the selvedge at center Front.

FINISHING

Sew Sleeves to selvedge edges of Vest armhole. *The armhole edging will roll around and cover the seam.*

Sew Sleeve seams.

Sew side seams with B, only taking half of edge stitches into seam allowances.

POCKET EDGINGS

On both sides of pocket fronts, work as follows.

With smallest needle and B, and with purl side facing, pick up and knit 1 stitch for every row along pocket edge—approximately 24 (26, 28) stitches.

Work 4 rows in RSS, beginning with a (WS) knit row and ending with a purl row. Bind off knitwise, leaving long tail for seaming.

With tail, sew bound-off edge to pocket front.

Sew upper and lower corners of pocket edgings down to Vest Front.

❋ TECHNIQUE ❋

Sometimes reverse stockinette edgings roll. If these do, wash the garment as directed in a wool-wash solution. Pin the front and back edgings together until the piece is dry. Fold the hood in half and pin both edges together until the piece is dry. This should counteract the roll of these edgings.

Vested Hoodie

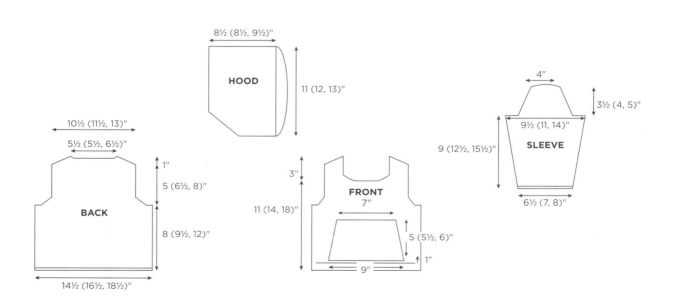

Baby's First Doll

DESIGNED BY SALLY

I watched Leila, my five-day-old granddaughter, absolutely transfixed—with unblinking calm—by black and white patterns and shapes. So here's the pattern for a doll I made for her—with arms that allow it to be hung or tied at the 8–12" (20.5-30.5cm) distance on which a new baby can focus. (My baby-expert friends assure me that the arms on this doll do not pose a choking hazard. But when not in use, the arms could be wrapped around the body and snapped shut. Or you could forego the arms-as-hangers option and simply make them shorter and without the snaps.)

SKILL LEVEL
Intermediate

SIZE
All measurements are approximate.
> Width (of body) 5" (12.5cm)
> Height 11¾" (30cm)

MATERIALS
> Sirdar Snuggly (55% nylon, 45% acrylic, each approximately 1¾ oz [50g] and 191yd [175m]), **(3)** light, in the following amounts and colors:
> 180yd (164m) / 1 ball, in color 0312 (black)
> 160yd (146m) / 1 ball, in color 0251 (white)
> One circular needle, size 5 (3.75mm), any length
> One set of 5 dpns, size 4 (3.5mm)
> Small piece of red or pink or orange yarn (with same washing instructions as doll yarn)
> One black snap, ½" (13mm) wide

GAUGE
Approximately 16 stitches and 32 rows = 4" (10cm) in lampshade stitch (in body of doll), over larger needles *Gauge does not matter.*

PATTERN NOTE
You don't need the circular needle to work any part of the doll, but it does make the neck ruffle easier to manage.

Doll

BODY
With black and larger needle, long-tail cast on 25 stitches.

Next 4 Rows With black, wyif slip 1 purlwise, k24.

Next Row (WS) With black, wyif sl 1 p-wise, k3; *take black to WS, with white p1; take white to WS, with black k3; repeat from * 4 times more to last stitch; with black k1.

INSPIRATION

If you choose, you could make this doll in any bright colors: red or yellow hair and/or body parts in any number of bright colors. The black and white is offered because it is rare to find something especially designed for our littlest ones who actually prefer black and white.

Next Row, Make Bobbles (RS) With black, wyif sl 1 p-wise, k3; *with white, kf&b&f&b into next (white) stitch, turn and k4, turn and p4, turn and k4, turn and sl 2 together p-wise, k2tog, pass 2 slip stitches over; take white to WS, with black, k3; repeat from * 4 times more to last stitch; with black k1. Cut white.

✳ TECHNIQUE ✳

Do not work in any tails unless indicated: knot them, and then tuck them inside to provide some of the stuffing. (A large portion of this yarn is used for stuffing: if you use other yarn for the stuffing, make sure the yarn has the same washing instructions as the doll's yarn.)

Next Row (WS) With black, wyif sl 1 p-wise, then knit all black stitches but bring yarn to front and sl 1 p-wise at all white stitches.
Next 4 Rows With black, wyif sl 1 p-wise, k24.
Next 2 RS Rows With black, sl 1 p-wise, k24.
Next 2 WS Rows With black, sl 1 p-wise, p24.
Do not cut yarns until indicated. Carry yarn not in use up side.
Lampshade Stitch, Row 1 (RS) With white, sl 1 p-wise, k3; insert right needle into stitch 4 rows below next stitch on left needle and k1 (1 dip stitch made), knit next stitch on left needle as usual, pass "dip stitch" over stitch just knit, k3; repeat from * 4 times more to last stitch, k1.
Rows 2 and 4 With white, sl 1 p-wise, p24.
Row 3 With white, sl 1 p-wise, k24.
Row 5 With black, sl 1 p-wise, k1; insert right needle into stitch 4 rows below next stitch on left needle and k1 (1 dip stitch made), knit next stitch on left needle as usual, pass "dip stitch" over stitch just knit, k3; repeat from * 4 times more; insert right needle into stitch 4 rows below next stitch on left needle and k1, knit next stitch on left needle as usual, pass "dip stitch" over stitch just knit, k2.
Rows 6 and 8 With black, sl 1 p-wise, p24.
Row 7 With black, sl 1 p-wise, k24.
Repeat these 8 rows (of lampshade stitch) 8 times more. Piece measures approximately 10" (25.5cm). Cut white.
Bind off in black, leaving long tail for seaming.
With tail, sew bound-off row to cast-on edge.

LEFT LEG

Fold Body so white bobbles sit at center front.
With black, dpns, and RS facing, begin at center front to pick up and knit 1 stitch in every slip stitch along the edge to center back—24 stitches.
**Distribute stitches evenly onto 4 dpns.
Knit 2 rounds in black.
*Work 3 rounds as follows and in white, then work 3 rounds as follows and in black.
Round 1 Knit.
Round 2 Slip first stitch purlwise, knit to end.
Round 3 Knit.

✳ TECHNIQUE ✳

The slip stitch (see Glossary, page 167) at the beginning of round 2 in a new color eliminates the jog at the color change.

Repeat from * twice more.
Cut black.
Work 3 rounds as above and in white.
Decrease Round K1, skp, knit to last 3 stitches of needle 2, k2tog, k1; k1, skp, knit to last 3 stitches of needle 4, k2tog, k1—5 stitches on each needle.
Knit 2 rounds in white.
Repeat decrease round twice more—3 stitches on each needle.
Cut white, and graft 6 stitches of needles 1 and 2 to 6 stitches of needles 3 and 4.

✳ TECHNIQUE ✳

If you don't know how to graft, just draw cut yarn through the remaining stitches to close the legs. Do the same with the arms.

RIGHT LEG

With black, dpns, and RS facing, begin at center back (and in same stitch as last stitch of Left Leg) to pick up and knit 1 stitch in every slip stitch at edge to center front—24 stitches.
Work as from ** to end of Left Leg.
Stuff the Legs with cut pieces of yarn.
Close the Legs by sewing across their tops where they attach to the Body.

✳ TECHNIQUE ✳

Sewing across the pieces after stuffing keeps their filling from migrating into other pieces.

ARMS (MAKE 2)

With black and 1 dpn, cast on 12 stitches.

Distribute stitches evenly over 4 dpns. Be careful not to twist cast-on edge.

Knit in rounds until Arm measures 7″ (18cm). Cut black. With white, knit 6 rounds.

Decrease Round [K1, skp, k2tog, k1] twice—2 stitches on each needle.

Cut white, and graft 4 stitches of needles 1 and 2 to 4 stitches of needles 3 and 4.

Sew the Arms securely onto black rows at the fold lines of the Body, 1″ (2.5cm) below the upper edge. *Do sew in the tails of the arms: they are not stuffed.*

HEAD

With white, dpns, and RS facing, begin at center back to pick up and knit 1 stitch in every slip stitch along the upper edge of the Body—approximately 46 stitches. Purl 1 round.

Knit in rounds until Head measures 2¾″ (7cm). Bind off.

With black, duplicate stitch eyes and nose as shown in chart.

For the mouth, work as follows: with small piece of colored yarn, wrap twice, loosely, around 3 stitches where shown on chart (½″ [13mm] below the nose); with remaining yarn, wrap around these pieces of yarn 5 or 6 times; bury tails.

The result will look like a bullion stitch. If you know how to do a bullion stitch, you could do this instead.

NECK RUFFLE (MADE IN 2 PIECES)

With white and larger needle, RS facing, and Doll upside down, begin at center front to pick up and knit 1 stitch in every purl stitch around the base of the Head to center back. Turn.

**Next Row (WS) [P1, yo, p1] in every stitch.

Knit 1 row, purl 1 row, knit 1 row. Cut white.

Next Row (WS) With black, purl.

Next Row *P1, yo; repeat from * to end.

Bind off knitwise.

With white and larger needle, RS facing, and Doll upside down, begin at center back to pick up and knit in every purl stitch around the base of the Head to center front. Turn.

Work as above from ** to end.

Sew the Neck Ruffles down at center front (so they do not obscure the mouth).

INSPIRATION

Use the long arms and snaps to attach the doll to the slats of a crib, to a mobile, to the handle of a stroller, to the headrest of a car (so the doll will be visible from the car seat), or around your neck. (If the head needs to be stabilized, thread the arms through the hair before hanging the doll.)

Baby's First Doll

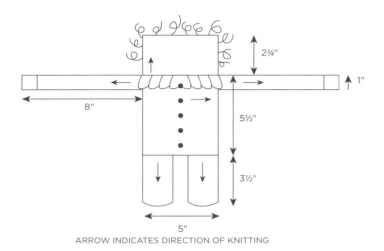

ARROW INDICATES DIRECTION OF KNITTING

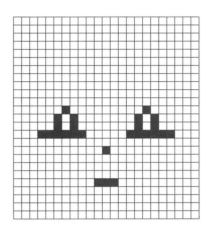

FINISHING

Stuff the Body with cut pieces of yarn.

Close the Body by sewing across the base of the Head just above the Neck Ruffles.

Stuff the Head with cut pieces of white yarn.

Close the Head by sewing its bound-off edges together and so the sides of the Head match the natural fold line of the Body.

Sew snap pieces very securely to Arms, onto the black just before the Arm changes to white.

HAIR (MAKE APPROXIMATELY 16 PIECES)

With black, work as follows.

- Cut a piece of yarn, approximately 36–48" (91–120cm)
- Fold the yarn (so it is doubled)
- Hold the 2 cut ends 4" (10cm) from the end
- Bring the fold from the other end back to this point, and take one of the cut ends through this fold (to secure it), then hold these pieces at this spot in one hand
- Insert a finger of your other hand into the fold at the other end, and spin your finger until the yarn is tightly spiraled

- Bring both hands together, and take one cut end through the fold at the end of the spiral (in order to secure it)
- Thread the cut ends onto a tapestry needle, and sew the hair securely onto the head
- While sewing subsequent pieces of hair, secure previous pieces as needed.

Sew most of the hair pieces along the top of the Head, but sew some to the upper back and some to the upper sides.

Kids' Sport Sweater

DESIGNED BY SALLY

I've never known children who didn't want to wear athletic gear—and teams are wearing some pretty wild pieces! I chose to work a rather simple version that wouldn't remind us of a particular team and that would be simple to work.

So for whatever child, whatever team, and in whatever colors, here is the classic sports pullover for him or her—and for the knitter who wants to give the sweater that will be truly appreciated and worn.

SKILL LEVEL
Intermediate

SIZES
> Child's 2-4 (6-8, 10-12)
> Finished chest 28 (32, 36)" (71 [81, 91]cm)
> Finished length (before washing) 15 (19, 22)" (38 [48.5, 56]cm)
> Finished length (after washing) 14 (18, 21)" (35.5 [45.5, 53.5]cm)
> Finished sleeve length (after washing) 18 (22, 26)" (45.5 [56, 66]cm)

Model is shown in size 6-8.

MATERIALS
> Brown Sheep Cotton Fleece (80% cotton, 20% merino wool, each approximately 3½ oz [100g] and 215yd [197m]) (4) medium, in the following amounts and colors:
> 220 (320, 520)yd (198 [288, 468]m) / 2 (2, 3) balls, in color 590 (lapis), A
> 150 (215, 344)yd (135 [197, 315]m) / 1 (1, 2) balls, in color 310 (wild orange), B
> 145 (210, 336)yd (132 [189, 300]m) / 1 (1, 2) balls, in color 005 (cavern), C
> 50yd (45m) / 1 ball, in color 100 (cotton ball), D
> One pair size 4 (3.5mm) needles
> One pair size 6 (4mm) needles, or size needed to obtain gauge
> 2 buttons, 7/16" (12mm) wide, in color to match collar
> Stitch holder

GAUGE
21 stitches and 28 stitches = 4" (10cm) in stockinette stitch, over larger needles and before washing

PATTERN NOTE
The garment has dark side panels (which are not obvious in the photos but are included in the finished measurement). They are knit separately and seamed. You could knit them in, in intarsia (see Glossary, page 167), but knitting them separately makes the work easier.

✳ FLATTER & FIT ✳

Sleeve length is measured from center body to end of sleeve. For more information, see Glossary, page 167.

Sweater

BACK
EDGING
With smaller needles and A, cast on 55 (65, 75) stitches.
RS Rows K1, *p1, k1; repeat from * to end.
WS Rows P1, *k1, p1; repeat from * to end.

✳ TECHNIQUE ✳
I like to do my ribbing over an odd number of stitches, because I find I get the best seams when I take half of each edge knit stitch into the seam allowance.

Work until edging measures 2" (5cm).

BODY
Change to larger needles, and work stockinette stitch until piece measures 7 (10, 12)" (18 [25.5, 30.5]cm). Cut A. (Shorten or lengthen for finished length here.)
The garment is made to 1" (2.5cm) longer than finished length, to allow for shrinkage.
Change to C, and work stockinette stitch until piece measures 9 (12, 14)" (23 [30.5, 35.5]cm). Cut C.
Change to B, and work stockinette stitch until piece measures 13 (17, 20)" (33 [43, 51]cm). Cut B.
Change to C, and work stockinette stitch until piece measures 14 (18, 21)" (35.5 [45.5, 53.5]cm). End after working a WS row.

SHAPE RIGHT BACK NECK
Knit to 14 (19, 24) stitches on right needle. Put center 27 stitches onto holder. Turn.
*Bind off 1 stitch at neck edge, work to end.

Work 1 row even.
Repeat the last 2 rows once more—12 (17, 22) stitches remain for shoulder.
Bind off on the next RS row.

SHAPE LEFT BACK NECK
Return to remaining 14 (19, 24) stitches, RS facing.
With C, work 2 rows.
Work as Shape Right Back Neck from * to end.

FRONT
Work as Back until piece measures 10 (14, 17)" (25.5 [35.5, 43]cm). End after working a WS row.

RIGHT FRONT
Knit to 26 (31, 36) stitches on right needle. Bind off next 3 stitches (for placket opening), knit to end. Continue over 26 (31, 36) stitches of Right Front until piece measures 12 (17, 21)" (30.5 [43, 53.5]cm). End after working a WS row.

SHAPE RIGHT FRONT NECK
Bind off 7 stitches at neck edge, work to end.
Work 1 row even. Cut B.
*Change to C, and continue to shape neck as follows.
Bind off 3 stitches at neck edge, work to end.
Work 1 row even.
Bind off 2 stitches at neck edge, work to end.
Work 1 row even.
Bind off 1 stitch at neck edge, work to end.
Work 1 row even.
Repeat the last 2 rows once—12 (17, 22) stitches in shoulder.
Work even until pieces measures the same length as Back. End after working a WS row.
Bind off.

LEFT FRONT
Return to remaining 26 (31, 36) stitches, RS facing. Continue over 26 (31, 36) stitches of Left Front until piece measures same length as Right Front to neck. End after working a RS row.

SHAPE LEFT FRONT NECK
Bind off 7 stitches at neck edge, work to end. Cut B.
Work as Shape Right Front Neck from * to end.

SIDE PANELS (MAKE 2)
EDGING
With C and smaller needles, cast on 23 stitches.
Work Edging as Back.

BODY

Change to larger needles.
Work in stockinette stitch to the same number of rows as Back where C stripe ends.
Bind off.

RIGHT SLEEVE

✳ TECHNIQUE ✳

I know lots of knitters who knit pick up and knit the sleeves down from the back and front, but I never had . . . until this garment. The reason I did it here was so that the maximum amount of color B could be used. Another good reason to do this is to knit the sleeves to the right length and then allow them to be easily lengthened as the child grows.

Sew right shoulder seam.
Divide remaining B into two equal amounts.
With larger needles and one amount of B, work as follows: take 1 stitch from the edge of the body pieces into the seam allowance; with RS facing, begin at the start of the B section of the Back to pick up and knit 5 stitches for every 7 rows to the shoulder seam and then down the Front to the end of the B section—approximately 58 (68, 78) stitches.
You don't need to get this exact number of stitches; you just need to get close. You do need to add 1 at each end of the next row.

*Next Row Purl, AT THE SAME TIME e-wrap cast on 1 stitch at beginning and end of row—60 (70, 80) stitches.

✳ TECHNIQUE ✳

The extra stitches are for seam allowances: if you do not add them, you'll get puckers at the underarms.

Work stockinette stitch for 4 more rows.
(Lengthen for Sleeve length here.)
The sleeves are made to 1" (2.5cm) longer than the finished sleeve length, to allow for shrinkage.
Decrease Row (RS) K1, skp, knit to last 3 stitches, k2tog, k1.
Work 5 rows even.
(Shorten for sleeve length by working fewer rows between decreases.)
Repeat the last 6 rows until you run out of this amount of B or have worked with B to desired length. Cut B.
Change to C, and continuing with a Decrease Row every 6th row, work 2" (5cm) in C. Cut C.
Change to A, and continuing with a Decrease Row every 6th row, work in A until Sleeve measures 12 (15, 18)" (30.5 [38, 45.5]cm)—approximately 34 (38, 40) stitches. End after working a WS row.

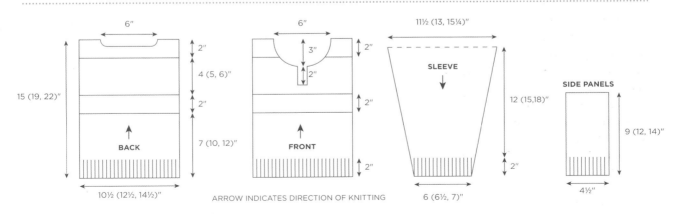

Kids' Sport Sweater

BACK — 6" / 2" / 4 (5, 6)" / 2" / 15 (19, 22)" / 7 (10, 12)" / 10½ (12½, 14½)"

FRONT — 6" / 3" / 2" / 2" / 2" / 2"

ARROW INDICATES DIRECTION OF KNITTING

SLEEVE — 11½ (13, 15¼)" / 12 (15,18)" / 2" / 6 (6½, 7)"

SIDE PANELS — 9 (12, 14)" / 4½"

CUFF

Decrease Row (RS) Knit, decreasing evenly across row to 31 (33, 37) stitches.

Beginning with a WS row, work 1x1 rib until Cuff measures 2″ (5cm).

Bind off in rib.

LEFT SLEEVE

Sew left shoulder seam.

With larger needles and B, work as follows: with RS facing, take 1 stitch from the edge of the body pieces into the seam allowance; begin at the start of the B section of the Front to pick up and knit 5 stitches for every 7 rows to the shoulder seam and then down the Back to the end of the B section—approximately 58 (68, 78) stitches.

Work as Right Sleeve from * to end.

FINISHING
✳ TECHNIQUE ✳

Since the collar and placket are done in white, the garment was washed (and dried in the dryer) *before* the collar and placket were added. This was done to release any dye exhaust so the colors of the garment would not bleed into the white with subsequent washings. If you work the collar and placket in a color, this pre-washing is likely not necessary.

Sew Side Panels to Front and Back.

Sew fronts of Sleeves to front of Side Panels, and sew backs of Sleeves to back of Side Panels (ending at center of Side Panels), then sew Sleeve seams as usual. If doing the plackets and collar in a lighter color, and if using the yarn indicated, wash the garment in cold water with detergent, and then add ½ cup (125mL) white vinegar to the rinse water. Dry as desired. *If you use a different yarn, wash and dry as directed by its label.*

RIGHT FRONT PLACKET

While the model garment shows the buttonholes on the girl side, the pattern is written with the buttonholes on the boy's side. Work buttonholes on the opposite placket for a girl's sweater.

With D and smaller needles, pick up and knit 5 stitches for every 6 rows along Right Front Neck opening—16 stitches.

Decrease or increase over the next row if you did not achieve 16 stitches.

WS Rows P2, *k1, p1; repeat from * to end.

RS Rows *K1, p1; repeat from * to last 2 stitches, k2.

Repeat these 2 rows until placket measures 1″ (2.5cm). Bind off in rib.

LEFT FRONT PLACKET

With D and smaller needles, pick up and knit 5 stitches for every 6 rows along Left Front neck opening—17 stitches.

Decrease or increase over the next row if you did not achieve 17 stitches.

WS Row P2, *k1, p1; repeat from * to last stitch, p1.

RS Row K2, *p1, k1; repeat from * to last stitch, k1.

Repeat WS row once.

Next Row, Make Buttonholes (RS) K2, p1, k1, yo, k2tog, [p1, k1] twice, yo, k2tog, p1, k1, p1, k2.

Work next WS row working yo's of buttonholes to avoid twisting them.

✳ TECHNIQUE ✳

It doesn't matter how you execute your buttonhole's yo (see Glossary, page 167) or how it is oriented for the next row. What is important is that you work the yo appropriately on the next row—in this case, not twisting it (which would make your buttonhole disappear). To not twist a yo, work through its *leading edge*—the part of the stitch closest to the tip of the needle.

Continue with rib as established until placket measures 1″ (2.5cm).

Bind off in rib.

Sew lower edge of Left Front placket down to bound-off edge at base of placket opening, taking 1 stitch from lower edge of this placket piece into seam allowance.

Sew lower edge of Right Front placket behind Left.

Sew buttons to Right Front placket to match placement of buttonholes.

COLLAR
✳ TECHNIQUE ✳

You may find the collar easier to work on a circular needle.

With smaller needles, color D, and RS facing, pick up and knit around neck edge as follows.

- 4 stitches from center of Right Front placket to edge of Right Front
- 1 stitch for every bound-off stitch,
- 1 stitch for every 2-row step between bound-off stitches

• 3 stitches for every 4 rows (along straight edges)
• 1 stitch for every stitch on holder
—approximately 97 stitches.

Next Row (WS) Wyif slip 1 purlwise, *k1, p1; repeat from * to last 2 stitches, k1, wyif slip 1 p-wise. AT THE SAME TIME, decrease to 89 stitches by p2tog in purls across Back neck.

RS Rows *K1, p1; repeat from * to last stitch, k1.

WS Rows Wyif sl 1 p-wise, *k1, p1; repeat from * to last 2 stitches, k1, wyif sl 1 p-wise.

Repeat the last 2 rows until collar measures 1¼" (3cm).

Change to larger needles and continue as established until Collar measures 2¾" (7cm).

Bind off in rib.

Steam-press the part of the collar done on larger needles (so it folds over nicely).

for
Family & Friends

Not all knit gifts are made for Christmas, but a chapter dedicated to gifts seems the right time and place to speak about knit gifts.

Canada's CBC radio once did a survey to discover the most-dreaded Christmas gift. It was, sadly, a hand-knit sweater. How can this be? How can something lovingly made be so under-appreciated?

I believe that some who answered were remembering the experience as a four-year old. And oh, my, it *was* traumatic—to have been given a *sweater* when what one wanted—*prayed for*—was some sort of muscle-bound figurine or weeping doll.

And then there may remain a few who had been presented with "the Christmas sweater." It was made for the right reasons but for the wrong person. Why? Because the person who did the knitting did what she (or he) wanted to knit, not what the recipient wanted to wear. And while many of us receive gifts we don't appreciate, it's difficult when it's something that requires *wearing*.

What is to be said about this? First and foremost, I believe that most of us are thrilled to receive a hand-knit item. And how can we ensure this?

If you are nervous about "the sweater," consider not making a garment. Make something for the home, or make an accessory.

If knitting something for the home, observe their home décor.

If making a full-sized garment, observe what the person actually wears. Can you knit something similar?

Make something classic—as we believe the clothing in this chapter to be.

Ask what sort of sweater this person would like—what style, what yarn, what color. Do this *especially* for someone between four and twenty.

Don't make sweaters for everyone every year. Choose only one person in the family to knit for. Make the gift of a sweater something to be anticipated.

If you give a four-year old a sweater, make sure *someone* is giving the muscle-bound figurine or weeping doll.   —SALLY

Argyle Watchband

DESIGNED BY CADDY

This may be my favorite pattern in the book. It's simple, quick, appropriate as a gift for just about anyone, makes use of your stash of leftover yarns, and is totally original. The first one I knit was for my friend Ben, who had found a vintage Toronto Blue Jays watch face and needed a watch band. He wears it so very well. Maybe you've seen him around? He's the guy with the Blue Jays watch and the matching argyle watchband.

SKILL LEVEL
Intermediate

SIZES
> One size
> Finished circumference (after seaming) 7½" (19cm)
> Finished width 2" (5cm)

MATERIALS
> 1 ball Classic Elite Classic One Fifty (100% fine merino, each approximately 1¾ oz [50g] and 150yd [135m]), (3) light, in the following amounts and colors:
> 10yd (9m), in color 7238 (chestnut) MC
> 6yd (5.5m), in color 7206 (sand) C1
> 2yd (1.8m), in color 7214 (elfin green) C2
> One pair size 2.5 (3mm) needles, or size needed to obtain gauge
> One watch face (with detachable pins), no more than 1½" (3.8cm) in diameter

GAUGE
30 stitches and 36 rows = 4" (10cm) in stockinette stitch

PATTERN NOTES
1. This watch band will fit most wrists; it has stretch and should not be made too big. Differences in sizes can be achieved by binding the edging off tightly or loosely.
2. To see this piece on a wrist, go to www.sallymelvilleknits.com and click on "Books."

Watchband

With MC, e-wrap cast on 13 stitches.

✳ TECHNIQUE ✳

You will work intarsia (see Glossary, page 167) in MC and C1, so use 2 lengths of MC and 1 length of C1. Cross these colors on wrong side at all color changes by always taking the color you have finished with over the color you are working with next. With C2 you have a choice: you can either knit it in, using 2 strands and carrying MC behind—as I did—or you can duplicate stitch it in at the end.

Beginning with row 1, work 13-stitch chart 3 times (to 60 rows), then repeat row 1.
The piece should not be loose on the wrist.
(Shorten or lengthen for finished circumference here.)
Bind off on the following WS row.

EDGING

With RS facing and MC, pick up and knit 2 stitches for every 3 rows along side edges.
Knit 1 row, then bind off knitwise.
For smaller wrists, bind off tightly; for larger wrists, bind off loosely.

FINISHING

Block well.
Sew the cast-on and bound-off edges together.
Remove the pins from the watch face.
Determine where you wish to place the watch face on the band.
You will want the watch face placed in such a way that your argyle pattern is symmetrical above and below it.
Slide one watch pin under 4 stitches, then attach it to one end of the watch face.
Lay the watch face flat, and slide the other pin under corresponding 4 stitches at the other end of the watch face, then attach it to the other end of the watch face.

Argyle Watchband

7½"

2"

☐ in MC, knit on RS rows, purl on WS rows

▨ in C1, knit on RS rows, purl on WS rows

⊟ in C2, knit on RS rows, purl on WS rows

19
17
15
13
11
9
7
5
3
1

Glasses Case

DESIGNED BY CADDY

While you could knit scarves and hats forever—and there are so many different and wonderful ways to create them—some of us may be looking for something else to knit as a gift.

This glasses case could be for a man or a woman, an adult or a child. And it certainly doesn't have to be a glasses case. Whatever you can think will fit, then that's what kind of a case it is. (It's perfect for that special someone who has always been looking for a case to hold her Barbie-doll-shoe collection!)

SKILL LEVEL
Easy

SIZE
All measurements are approximate.
> One size
> Finished width (before felting) 10½" (26.5cm)
> Finished height (before felting) 15½" (39.5cm)
For final measurement, see pattern notes and schematic

MATERIALS
> Patons Classic Wool (100% wool, each approximately 3½ oz [100g] and 223yd [205m]), (4) medium, in the following amounts and colors:
> 35yd (32m) / 1 ball in color 205 (deep olive) MC
> 20yd (18m) / 1 ball each in colors 218 (peacock) CC1, 240 (leaf green) CC2, 212 (royal purple) CC3
> One pair size 10 ¾ (7mm) needles
> One button, 1" (2.5cm) wide

GAUGE
Approximately 16 stitches and 24 rows = 4" (10cm) in stitch pattern, before felting
Gauge does not matter.

PATTERN NOTE
The schematic is a guideline for your finished measurements: you may trim your case as you desire.

Case

With MC, long-tail cast on 40 stitches.
Knit 1 (WS) row.
Work stitch pattern, with 2 rows in MC and then 4 rows in CC, as follows.
*You may use any number of CCs and in any order:
I used three and repeated them in order.*
Rows 1 and 2 With MC, knit.

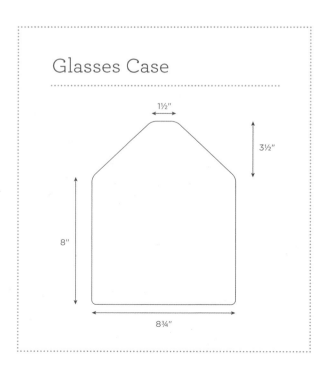

Glasses Case

1½"

3½"

8"

8¾"

Rows 3 and 5 With CC, *k3, sl 1 p-wise; repeat from * to last 4 stitches, k4.

Rows 4 and 6 With CC, p4, *sl 1 p-wise, k3; repeat from * to end.

Rows 7 and 8 With MC, knit.

Rows 9 and 11 With CC, k1, sl 1 p-wise, *k3, sl 1 p-wise; repeat from * to last 2 stitches, k2.

Rows 10 and 12 With CC, p2, sl 1 p-wise, *p3, sl 1 p-wise; repeat from * to last stitch, p1.

Work stitch pattern to 60 rows (5 repeats). AT THE SAME TIME change CCs for every stockinette stitch section. End after working row 12.

✳ TECHNIQUE ✳

There is no need to cut your yarn between color changes; it can be carried up the side. (Even if it's unattractive, remember you'll be cutting the sides to shape.) But do this very loosely, or you may distort the edge of the piece. And you don't need to worry about working in tails either: again, the edges of the piece will be cut to shape.

FLAP

Maintain stitch and color patterns through what follows.
Work row 1 (in MC).

Row 2 (Decrease, WS) Ssk, knit to last 2 stitches, k2tog.

Row 3 (Decrease, RS) Ssk, knit to last 2 stitches, k2tog.

Work rows 4 even.

Continue shaping piece as follows.

Work RS Decrease Row every RS CC row (rows 3, 5, 9, 11), and work WS Decrease Row every WS MC row (rows 2, 8) until 12 stitches remain. End after working a WS row.

Next (RS) Row, Make Buttonhole Work 5 stitches in pattern, yo, k2tog, work to end.

On the next row, be sure to not twist the yo of the buttonhole.

Work 4 rows (with 2 more Decrease Rows as established—8 stitches remain), then bind off.

FINISHING

Felt by putting case through one regular warm wash cycle of washing machine. Tumble in dryer on regular heat until dry.

Trim case along all sides to correspond with schematic (or to desired shape and size).

EDGING

Fold case in half so cast-on edge meets the first WS row of flap.

With MC, and beginning at bottom right, work blanket stitch (through both layers) to close the right side of the glasses case, around the single layer of the flap, and then down the left side of the case (through both layers).

Attach button to correspond to buttonhole.

My First Lace Scarf

DESIGNED BY SALLY

I wish I could call this an "easy" pattern, but lace—any lace—is considered by all knitting teachers and knitting books and knitting authorities to be "intermediate." Having said that, because this is only a six-stitch and eight-row repeat, I think it is easier to manage than most. And in spite of that, I think it looks more complicated than it is. Isn't that what we would wish from a first lace scarf?

SKILL LEVEL
Intermediate

SIZE
All measurements are approximate.
> Width 8" (20.5cm)
> Length 72" (183cm)

MATERIALS
> 495yd (450m) / 1 skein Curious Creek Fibers Meru (51% tussah silk, 49% merino, each approximately 1¾oz [50g] and 495yd [450m]), in color yellow brick road, lace
> One pair size 5 (3.75mm) needles

GAUGE
Approximately 21 stitches and 26 rows = 4" (10cm) in lace
Gauge does not matter.

✳ TECHNIQUE ✳
If this is your first lace, I would advise the following.
1. Choose a heavier-weight yarn (DK) rather than the lighter-weight yarn (lace) shown here.
2. Work with a "life line" as follows: thread a tapestry needle with thread or yarn, and weave it through all the stitches of row 1 while the stitches of that row are still on the needle; when you finish the following row 1, remove the life line and then re-insert it in the new row 1. This helps if you need to rip back, because then you have a safe place to land!
3. Count stitches as you work wrong-side rows.
4. Before you begin the lace of every row, look at the stitches and try to "read" your knitting. The sooner you learn to do this—anticipate rather than be a slave to the written directions—the more you will enjoy knitting lace.
5. Steam-press the piece often: this sometimes reveals errors that are not otherwise obvious.

Scarf
Long-tail cast on 43 stitches.
Next 3 Rows Wyif slip 1 purlwise, knit to end.
For all following directions, wyif slip 1 purlwise will be written as "sl 1."
Following Rows Beginning with row 1, work from chart or from following written directions.
Row 1 (RS) Sl 1, k3, *yo, skp, k1, k2tog, yo, k1; repeat from * to last 3 stitches, k3.

My First Lace Scarf

[6-STITCH REPEAT]

☐ knit on RS, purl on WS ╲ skp (or ssk)
● knit on WS ╱ k2tog
— wyif sl 1 p-wise ○ yo
⤬ sk2p

All WS Rows Sl 1, k2, p37, k3.
Row 3 Sl 1, k3, *yo, k1, sk2p, k1, yo, k1; repeat from * to last 3 stitches, k3.
Row 5 Sl 1, k3, *k2tog, yo, k1, yo, skp, k1; repeat from * to last 3 stitches, k3.
Row 7 Sl 1, k2, k2tog, *[k1, yo] twice, k1, sk2p; repeat from * to last 8 stitches, [k1, yo] twice, k1, skp, k3.

✳ TECHNIQUE ✳
The ssk is considered the industry standard for a left-leaning decrease. But I prefer the older skp (as do about half the students in my classes). (For full descriptions, see the Glossary, page 167.) It doesn't matter which you use, as long as you understand that the ssk or skp leans left and the k2tog leans right.

Repeat the 8 rows of this lace pattern until not less than 100" (255cm) yarn remains after working a RS row.
Next 3 Rows Sl 1, knit to end.
Bind off loosely.
Steam-press flat.

Lace Bookmarks

DESIGNED BY SALLY

So many knitters are also readers. Knowing that I am one, many years ago a dear friend surprised me with a beautiful lace bookmark. It's such a precious thing and such a gift to combine both loves.

What follows are three versions, one for each level of knitter. The experienced version was simple to develop: the most challenge came in working out the easiest version. (From left: Small Drop Lace Bookmark, Slanted Lace Bookmark, Open Heart Lace Bookmark.)

SKILL LEVEL
> Easy-Intermediate (Slanted Lace Bookmark)
> Intermediate (Small Drop Lace Bookmark)
> Experienced (Open Heart Lace Bookmark)

SIZES
All versions
> Width 1¾" (4.5cm)
> Height 8" (20.5cm)

MATERIALS
> 25yd (22.5m) / 1 spool Goldschild or Londonderry Linen Thread nel 80/3 (100% linen, each approximately 390yd [350m]), in color 15 (ivory), 🔟 lace
> One pair size 000 (1.5mm) needles, or size needed to obtain gauge
> Row counter
> Plastic bookmark sleeve, 2" (5cm) wide
> Thin metal ruler, less than 2" (5cm) wide

GAUGE
> Number of stitches in each piece = 1¾" (4.5cm) in lace pattern of each piece
> 60–66 rows = 4" (10cm) in lace pattern
> Stitch gauge matters because the piece need to fits in its plastic sleeve: row gauge is approximate and does not matter.

PATTERN NOTES
1. The yarn used is actually finer than 🔟 lace, but it is heavier than sewing thread.
2. The needle size suggested is usually only available in double-pointed needles.

✳ TECHNIQUE ✳
1. No matter how experienced you are, this project is not done quickly. The first row after the cast-on is especially challenging: don't be discouraged by it.
2. The linen thread does not have any elasticity, which can take some getting used to.
3. The stitches should sit loosely on the needles because this is meant to be open work. Like most lace work, this is both its beauty and its challenge.
4. The garter stitches at the edges of the two easier versions are difficult to make perfectly neat: I think their idiosyncrasies add to the hand-knit charm.

Bookmarks

SLANTED LACE BOOKMARK
Long-tail cast on 14 stitches.

✳ TECHNIQUE ✳
It is the tension on the "thumb" yarn—not the size of the needle—that determines the tightness of the long-tail cast-on. So to cast on loosely, do not pull the "thumb" yarn too tightly.

Next 4 Rows Knit.
Rows 1, 3, 5, 7, 9, 11 P2, [yo, p2tog] 5 times, p2.

If you wonder why stitch patterns like this are written with mostly p2tog's rather than k2tog's, it's that the direction of the needle makes p2tog easier to execute.

Rows 2, 4, 6, 8, 10 Purl.

This stitch pattern slants right and then left. It is essential to count rows and to work an 11- (not 12-) row repeat. Repeating over an odd number of rows makes the slant change direction.

Repeat these 11 rows until the piece measures approximately 7¾″ (19.5cm). End after working row 11.

Next 4 Rows Knit.

Bind off loosely.

FINISHING

Sew in tails as invisibly as possible.

Steam-press on linen setting.

With the ruler, slide the knit piece into the bookmark sleeve.

Trim the ends of the sleeve to suit.

SMALL DROP LACE BOOKMARK

Long-tail cast on 19 stitches.

Cast on loosely by not pulling the "thumb" yarn too tightly.

Next 5 Rows Knit.

Following Rows Beginning with row 1, work from small drop lace chart or with following written directions.

✳ TECHNIQUE ✳

The sk2p, used in this bookmark, is a left-leaning double decrease. The k3tog is a right-leaning double decrease. The s2kp, used in the final bookmark, is a centered double decrease. They are interchangeable in their function—in that they take 3 stitches down to 1—so you can use whichever of these three is most comfortable and whose look you prefer.

Row 1 (RS) K4, *yo, skp, k1, k2tog, yo, k1; repeat from * once, k3.

All WS Rows K3, p13, k3.

Row 3 K4, *yo, k1, sk2p, k1, yo, k1; repeat from * once, k3.

Row 5 K4, *k2tog, yo, k1, yo, skp, k1; repeat from * once, k3.

Row 7 K3, k2tog, [k1, yo] twice, k1, sk2p, [k1, yo] twice, k1, skp, k3.

Repeat 8 rows of small drop lace until piece measures approximately 7¾" (19.5cm). End after working row 8.

Next 6 Rows Knit.

Bind off loosely.

See Finishing (page 51, following Slanted Lace Bookmark).

OPEN HEART LACE BOOKMARK

I call this "open heart," because that's what it looks like to me when viewed upside down.

Long-tail cast on 21 stitches.

Cast on loosely by not pulling the "thumb" yarn too tightly.

Next 3 Rows Wyif slip 1 purlwise, k20.

Do not worry if the edge stitches are loose: you will tidy them at the end.

Slip all following slip stitches wyif and purlwise. Further directions will read "sl 1."

Following Rows Beginning with row 1, work from open heart lace chart or with following written directions.

✳ TECHNIQUE ✳

The k2togs can be difficult: Try slipping the right needle purlwise into the 2 stitches to be knit together and to stretch them open before working the k2tog as usual.

Row 1 (RS) Sl 1, k1, k2tog, yo, k1, yo, k3, skp, k1, k2tog, k3, yo, k1, yo, skp, k2.

All WS Rows Sl 1, k1, purl to last 2 stitches, k2.

Row 3 Sl 1, k1, [k2tog, yo] twice, k2, skp, k1, k2tog, k2, [yo, skp] twice, k2.

Row 5 Sl 1, k1, k2tog, [yo, k1] 3 times, skp, k1, k2tog, [k1, yo] 3 times, skp, k2.

Row 7 Sl 1, k1, [k2tog, yo] 3 times, skp, k1, k2tog, [yo, skp] 3 times, k2.

Row 9 Sl 1, k1, k2tog, yo, k4, yo, s2kp, yo, k4, yo, skp, k2.

Row 11 Sl 1, k3, yo, k11, yo, k4.

Repeat 12 rows of open heart lace until piece measures approximately 7¾" (19.5cm), End after working row 11.

Next 4 Rows Sl 1, k20.

Next (WS) Row Bind off loosely and in purl.

Optional To finish the slip-stitch edges, work as follows: slip needle through inside edges of slip stitches, introduce yarn, then—with RS facing—bind off loosely in knit. Do be careful to do this very loosely, or the edge will be too tight, which will cause the bookmark to be shorter and wider and to not fit into the sleeve as indicated.

See Finishing (page 51, following Slanted Lace Bookmark).

Lace Bookmarks

SMALL DROP LACE

	wyif sl 1 p-wise		ssk		sk2p
	knit on RS, purl on WS		k2tog		no stitch
•	knit on WS	◯	yo		s2kp

OPEN HEART LACE

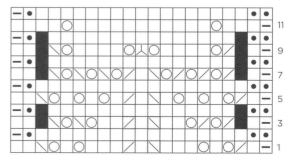

Andy's Polo

DESIGNED BY CADDY

Ever since I saw a knit polo shirt on Brad Pitt in the movie *Mr. and Mrs. Smith,* I have been searching for one just like it for my husband. They are harder to find than you'd think. Sure, I found designer ones for a few hundred dollars, but why on earth would I spend that much on a sweater when I can spend the money on yarn and knit it myself?

Inspired by one part Brad Pitt and three parts my husband, Andy, the result is a fitted polo shirt without too much polish (polish being the Brad Pitt part). The stitch pattern gives it some roughness, and the cuffs and edgings are done in rib but *not* on smaller needles, to give the finished sweater a subtle sloppy look (that being the Andy part). Just kidding: love you, babe.

SKILL LEVEL
Intermediate

SIZES
> S (M, L, 1X, 2X)
> Finished chest 38 (43, 45, 50, 55)" (96.5 [109, 114, 127, 139.5] cm)
> Finished length 27½ (28, 28½, 29, 29½)" (70 (71, 72, 74, 75] cm)
> Finished shoulder width 16½" (42cm)
> Finished sleeve length (with cuff folded back) 33 (33½, 34, 34½, 35)" (84 [85, 86, 87.5, 88.5] cm)

Model is shown in size M.

＊ FLATTER & FIT ＊

Sleeve length is measured from center body to end of sleeve. For more information, see Glossary, page 167.

MATERIALS

> 1605 (1785, 1965, 2140, 2320)yd (1445 [1605, 1770,
  1925, 2090]m) / 12 (13, 14, 16, 17) balls Rowan Classic Cashsoft DK (57% extra fine merino, 33% acrylic,
  10% cashmere, each approximately 1¾oz [50g] and
  142yd [130m]), in color 517 (donkey), (4) medium
> One pair size 8 (5mm) needles, or size needed to
  obtain gauge
> 2 stitch holders
> 3 buttons, ½" (13mm) wide

GAUGE

20 stitches and 30 rows = 4" (10cm) in Modified Linen
Stitch

STITCH PATTERN

Modified Linen Stitch (over a multiple of 3 + 1 stitch)
Row 1 *K1, wyif sl 2 purlwise; repeat from * to last 2
stitches, k2.
Row 2 Purl.
Row 3 K2, *wyif sl 2 purlwise; k1, repeat from * to end.
Row 4 Purl.

Polo

BACK

Cast on 97 (109, 115, 127, 139) stitches.
Work 1x1 rib, beginning and ending RS rows with k1

and WS rows with p1, for 3½" (9cm).
Beginning with row 1, work stitch pattern until piece
measures 18" (45.5cm). End after working a WS row.
(Shorten or lengthen for finished length here.)

SHAPE ARMHOLE

Bind off 3 (5, 7, 9, 12) stitches at the beginning of the
next 2 rows—91 (99, 101, 109, 115) stitches.
Decrease Row (RS) K1, ssk, work stitch pattern to last
3 stitches, k2tog, k1.

Work 3 (1, 1, 1, 1) rows even.
Repeat the last 4 (2, 2, 2, 2) rows 3 (7, 8, 12, 15) times
more—83 stitches.
(Widen or narrow for shoulder width by working fewer
or more decreases.)
Continue even until armhole measures 8½ (9, 9½, 10,
10½)" (21.5 [23, 24, 25.5, 26.5]cm). End after working
a WS row.

SHAPE RIGHT SHOULDER AND NECK

Next Row (RS) Bind off 6 stitches, work to 21 stitches
on right needle. Turn, leaving remaining 56 stitches on
needle for Back neck and left shoulder.
*Bind off 1 stitch at neck edge, work to end.
Bind off 6 stitches at armhole edge, work to end.
Repeat from * once—7 stitches.
Work 1 row even, then bind off final 7 stitches at
armhole edge.

SHAPE LEFT SHOULDER AND NECK

Put center 29 stitches on holder for neck.

Work 1 RS row over remaining 27 stitches.

Bind off 6 stitches at armhole edge, work to end.

Work as Shape Right Shoulder and Neck from * to end.

FRONT

Work as Back to Shape Armhole. End after working a WS row.

SHAPE ARMHOLE

Bind off 3 (5, 7, 9, 12) stitches at beginning of next 2 rows—91 (99, 101, 109, 115) stitches.

Decrease Row (RS) K1, ssk, work to last 3 stitches, k2tog, k1.

Work 3 (1, 1, 1, 1) rows even.

Repeat the last 4 (2, 2, 2, 2) rows 3 (7, 8, 12, 15) times more—83 stitches.

(Widen or narrow for shoulder width as Back.) Continue without decreases until armhole measures 3½ (4, 4½, 5, 5½)" (9 [10, 11.5, 12.5, 14]cm). End after working a WS row.

RIGHT FRONT

Next Row (RS) Work stitch pattern to 39 stitches on right needle; put these 39 stitches on holder. Continuing on same row, bind off the next 5 stitches (for placket opening), work to end.

Continue even on these 39 stitches until placket opening measures 4" (10cm). End after working a WS row.

SHAPE RIGHT NECK

Shape neck by binding off at neck edge as follows: 6 stitches once, 2 stitches twice, then 1 stitch 4 times—25 stitches.

Work even until armhole measures same as Back. End after working a RS row.

SHAPE RIGHT SHOULDER

Bind off 6 stitches at armhole edge, work to end.

Work 1 row even.

Repeat the last 2 rows twice more, then bind off remaining stitches.

LEFT FRONT

Return to stitches on holder for Left Front, ready to work a WS row.

Continue even on these 39 stitches until placket opening measures same as Right Front. End after working a RS row.

SHAPE LEFT NECK

Work as Shape Right Neck. End after working a WS row.

SHAPE LEFT SHOULDER

Work as Shape Right Shoulder.

SLEEVES

Cast on 54 (54, 54, 58, 58) stitches.

Work 1x1 rib for 3½" (9cm), increasing 1 stitch in last row for sizes S (M, L) only—55 (55, 55, 58, 58) stitches.

Andy's Polo

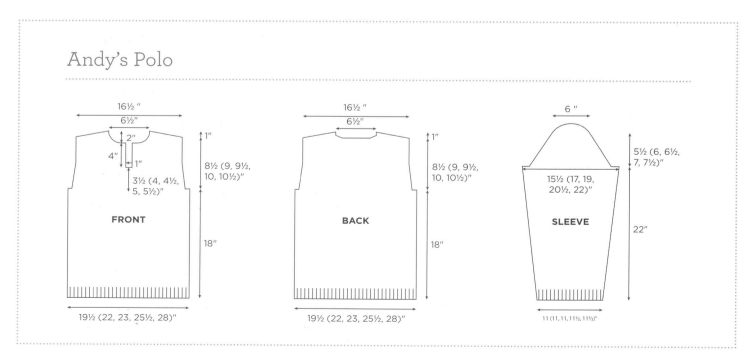

FRONT

16½"
6½"
2"
4"
1"
1"
3½ (4, 4½, 5, 5½)"
8½ (9, 9½, 10, 10½)"
18"
19½ (22, 23, 25½, 28)"

BACK

16½"
6½"
1"
8½ (9, 9½, 10, 10½)"
18"
19½ (22, 23, 25½, 28)"

SLEEVE

6"
5½ (6, 6½, 7, 7½)"
15½ (17, 19, 20½, 22)"
22"
11 (11, 11, 11½, 11½)"

End after working a WS row.
Beginning with row 1, work stitch pattern for 8 (4, 4, 2, 2) rows.

Increase Row (RS) K1, increase 1 in next stitch, work to last 2 stitches, increase 1 in next stitch, k1.

✳ TECHNIQUE ✳

Maintain stitch pattern by working more knit stitches or by slipping just 1 stitch purlwise. But for neat seams, always work the Increase Row as written.

Work 9 (5, 5, 3, 3) rows even.
Repeat the last 10 (6, 6, 4, 4) rows 11 (15, 19, 21, 25) times more—79 (87, 95, 102, 110) stitches. Continue even until sleeve measures 22" (56cm). End after working a WS row.
(Shorten or lengthen for finished sleeve length here.)

SHAPE SLEEVE CAP

Bind off 3 (5, 7, 9, 12) stitches at the beginning of the next 2 rows—73 (77, 81, 84, 86) stitches.

Decrease Row (RS) K1, ssk, work to last 3 stitches, k2tog, k1.
Purl 1 row.
Repeat the last 2 rows 19 (21, 23, 25, 26) times more—33 (33, 33, 32, 32) stitches.
Bind off 2 stitches at beginning of next 2 rows.
Bind off 4 stitches at beginning of next 2 rows.
Bind off remaining stitches.

FINISHING

Sew shoulder seams.
Sew Sleeves into armholes.
Sew side and Sleeve seams.

RIGHT PLACKET EDGING

With RS facing and beginning at bottom of Right Front placket opening, pick up and knit 2 stitches for every 3 rows along edge—approximately 25 stitches.

Across the next row, increase or decrease evenly (as needed) to 25 stitches.
Beginning WS rows with k1, work 1x1 rib for 1¼" (3cm).
End after working a RS row.
Bind off in rib.

LEFT PLACKET EDGING

With RS facing and beginning at top of Left Front placket opening, pick up and knit as Right Placket Edging.
Beginning WS rows with k1, work 1x1 rib for ½" (13mm).
End after working a WS row.

Next (RS) Row, Make Buttonholes [P1, k1] twice, yo, k2tog, *[p1, k1] 3 times, yo, k2tog; repeat from * once, p1, k1, p1.
On the next row, work yo to not twist it.
Continue working 1x1 rib to 1¼" (3cm). End after working a RS row.
Bind off in rib.

COLLAR

✳ TECHNIQUE ✳

You might find it easier to work the collar on a circular needle.

With RS facing and beginning in middle of Right Front placket edging, pick up and knit as follows:

- 2 stitches for every 3 rows (along straight edges)
- 1 stitch for every bound-off stitch
- 1 stitch for every 2-row step between bound-off stitches
- 1 stitch for every stitch on holder

—end in middle of Left Front placket edging, approximately 103 stitches.
Be sure to have an odd number of stitches.
Beginning WS rows with p1, work 1x1 rib for 3 rows.

Increase Row (RS) K1, increase 1 in next stitch, work to last 2 stitches, increase 1 in next stitch, k1.
Work 3 rows even in rib.
Purl first 2 and last 2 stitches on WS rows (and knit them on RS rows) for rows worked even following the 1st, 3rd, 5th, and 7th Increase Rows.
Repeat the last 4 rows until the collar measures 4¼" (11cm). End after working a WS row.
Bind off in pattern.

Sew lower edge of left placket edging to placket bound-off edge.
Sew lower edge of right placket edging behind right.
Sew buttons to Right Front placket to correspond to placement of buttonholes.

The Cardigan Caddy Really Wanted

DESIGNED BY CADDY

I asked for lots of boring sweaters when I was younger—pullovers, turtlenecks, and cardigans, all done in solid colors and without (God forbid!) any texture. I know what you're thinking: asking Sally Melville to knit plain sweaters is like asking Van Gogh if he wouldn't mind coming over and painting your bathroom beige. So of course what I ended up with was a pullover with multi-colored converse shoes all over it, a turtleneck covered in brightly colored fish, and a cardigan intricately textured with cables, bobbles, and flowers. (This was the '80s!)

I have since seen the error of my ways and now know that if I want something plain I better darn well knit it myself! So here is the version of the cardigan I really wanted. Boring to knit? Maybe for some. But I bet you'll wear it every day.

SKILL LEVEL
Intermediate

SIZES
> XS (S, M, L, 1X)
> Finished bust 31 (35½, 40½, 45, 49)" (79 [90, 103, 114, 124.5] cm)
> Finished length 19½ (20, 21, 21½, 22)" (49.5 [51, 53.5, 54.5, 56] cm)
> Finished shoulder width 12 (13¼, 14½, 15¾, 16½)" (30.5 [33.5, 37, 40, 42] cm)
> Finished sleeve length 28 (28¾, 30, 31¾, 32¾)" (71 [73, 76, 80.5, 83] cm)

Model is shown in size XS.

✳ FLATTER & FIT ✳

Sleeve length is measured from center body to end of sleeve. For more information, see Glossary, page 167.

MATERIALS
> 1230 (1355, 1480, 1600, 1720)yd (1105 [1220, 1335, 1440, 1550]m) / 10 (11, 12, 12, 13) balls Nashua Cilantro (70% cotton, 30% polyester, each approximately 1¾oz [50g] and 136yd [125m]), in color NCIL011 (delft blue), ④ medium
> One pair size 9 (5.5mm) needles, or size needed to obtain gauge
> 5 or 6 buttons, ½" (13mm) wide

GAUGE
> 18 stitches and 28 rows = 4" (10cm) in stockinette stitch
> 20 stitches and 28 rows = 4" (10cm) in faux cable

STITCH PATTERNS
1x2 Rib (over a multiple of 3 + 2 stitches)

✳ TECHNIQUE ✳
I believe it is standard to describe rib as follows: the number of knit stitches followed by the number of purl stitches. Hence, this k1, p2 rib is described as 1x2 rib.

RS Rows P2, *k1, p2; repeat from * to end.
WS Rows K2, *p1, k2; repeat from * to end.

Faux Cable (over a multiple of 6 + 2 stitches)

✳ TECHNIQUE ✳

I call this stitch pattern "faux cable" because the stitch pattern gives the illusion of a cable without actually moving stitches around. It's a big-bang-for-your-buck stitch pattern. We didn't offer a chart because the written pattern is so simple.

Rows 1, 3, and 5 *P2, k4; repeat from * to last 2 stitches, p2.
Rows 2, 4, and 6 K2, *p4, k2; repeat from * to end.
Rows 7, 9, and 11 *K3, p2, k1; repeat from * to last 2 stitches, k2.
Rows 8, 10, and 12 P2, *p1, k2, p3; repeat from * to end.

Cardigan

BACK
Long-tail cast on 71 (80, 89, 98, 107) stitches.
Work 1x2 rib for 1¾" (4.5cm). End after working a WS row.
Work in stockinette stitch until piece measures 12" (30.5cm). End after working a WS row.
(Shorten or lengthen for finished length here.)

SHAPE ARMHOLE
Bind off 4 (5, 6, 7, 8) stitches at beginning of next 2 rows—63 (70, 77, 84, 91) stitches.
Decrease Row (RS) K1, ssk, knit to last 3 stitches, k2tog, k1.

✳ TECHNIQUE ✳

I have been taught to use the ssk for my left-leaning decrease. (It is, apparently, considered the industry standard.) I know that my mom continues to prefer the older skp. It doesn't matter which you use, as long as you understand that the ssk or skp leans left and the k2tog leans right. (See Glossary, page 167.)

Purl 1 row.
Repeat the last 2 rows 3 (4, 5, 6, 7) times more—55 (60, 65, 70, 75) stitches.
(Widen or narrow for shoulder width by working fewer or more decreases.)
Work even until armhole measures 6½ (7, 8, 8½, 9)" (16.5 [18, 20.5, 21.5, 23]cm). End after working a WS row.

SHAPE RIGHT SHOULDER AND NECK
Next Row (RS) Bind off 3 (3, 4, 4, 5) stitches, work to 11 (13, 14, 16, 17) stitches on right needle. Put center 27 (28, 29, 30, 31) stitches on holder (for Back neck). Turn.
**Next Row Bind off 1 stitch at neck edge, work to end.
Next Row Bind off 3 (4, 4, 4, 5) stitches at armhole edge, work to end.
Next Row Bind off 1 stitch at neck edge, work to end.
Next Row Bind off 3 (3, 4, 4, 5) stitches at armhole edge, work to end.**
On next RS row, bind off remaining stitches.

SHAPE LEFT SHOULDER AND NECK

Work 1 RS row over remaining 14 (16, 18, 20, 22) stitches.

Next Row (WS) Bind off 3 (4, 4, 5, 5) stitches at armhole edge, work to end.

Work as Shape Right Shoulder and Neck from ** to **. On the next WS row, bind off remaining stitches.

LEFT FRONT

Cast on 38 (44, 50, 56, 62) stitches.

Work 1x2 rib for 1¾" (4.5cm). End after working a WS row.

Beginning with row 1 of faux cable, work until piece measures same as Back to armhole. End after working a WS row.

SHAPE ARMHOLE

Maintain stitch pattern as established through all following shaping.

Next Row (RS) Bind off 4 (5, 7, 8, 10) stitches, work to end—34 (39, 43, 48, 52) stitches.

✳ TECHNIQUE ✳

There are slightly more stitches in the front underarm bind-offs and shoulders than the back because of its slightly narrower stitch gauge. You will address this when seaming.

Work 1 row even.

Decrease Row (RS) K1, ssk, work to end.

Work 1 row even.

Repeat last 2 rows 3 (4, 6, 7, 9) times more—30 (34, 36, 40, 42) stitches.

(Widen or narrow for shoulder width by working fewer or more decreases.)

Work even until armhole measures 4½ (5, 6, 6½, 7)" (11.5 [12.5, 15, 16.5, 18]cm). End after working a RS row.

SHAPE NECK

Bind off at neck edge as follows: 7 (9, 8, 10, 10) stitches once, 3 stitches once, 2 stitches twice, then 1 stitch 3 times—13 (15, 18, 20, 22) stitches.

Work even until armhole measures same as Back to shoulder. End after working a WS row.

SHAPE SHOULDER

Bind off at shoulder edge as follows: 3 (3, 4, 5, 5) stitches once, 3 (4, 5, 5, 6) stitches once, 3 (4, 4, 5, 5) stitches once, then 4 (4, 5, 5, 6) stitches—0 stitches.

The Cardigan Caddy Really Wanted

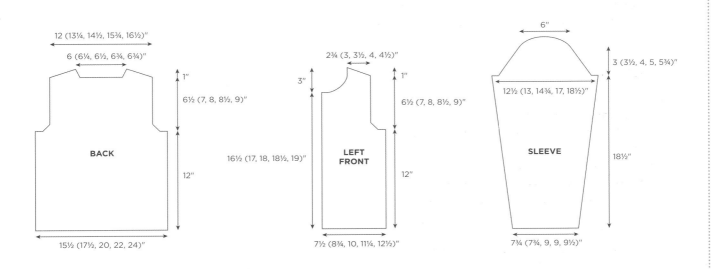

BACK

12 (13¼, 14½, 15¾, 16½)"
6 (6¼, 6½, 6¾, 6¾)"
1"
6½ (7, 8, 8½, 9)"
16½ (17, 18, 18½, 19)"
12"
15½ (17½, 20, 22, 24)"

LEFT FRONT

2¾ (3, 3½, 4, 4½)"
3"
1"
6½ (7, 8, 8½, 9)"
12"
7½ (8¾, 10, 11¼, 12½)"

SLEEVE

6"
3 (3½, 4, 5, 5¾)"
12½ (13, 14¾, 17, 18½)"
18½"
7¾ (7¾, 9, 9, 9½)"

RIGHT FRONT

Work as Left Front to armhole. End after working a RS row.

SHAPE ARMHOLE

Maintain stitch pattern as established through all following shaping.

Next Row (WS) Bind off 4 (5, 7, 8, 10) stitches, work to end—34 (39, 43, 48, 52) stitches.

Decrease Row (RS) Knit to last 3 stitches, k2tog, k1. Work 1 row even.

Repeat last 2 rows 3 (4, 6, 7, 9) times more—30 (34, 36, 40, 42) stitches.

(Widen or narrow for shoulder width as Left Front.) Work even until armhole measures same length as Left Front. End after working a WS row.

SHAPE NECK

Work as Left Front, Shape Neck. End after working a RS row.

SHAPE SHOULDER

Work as Left Front, Shape Shoulder.

SLEEVES

Cast on 35 (35, 41, 41, 43) stitches.

Work 1x2 rib for 1¾" (4.5cm). End after working a WS row.

Work 4 rows in stockinette stitch.

Continue in stockinette stitch for duration of Sleeve.

Increase Row (RS) K1, work lifted increase in next stitch, knit to last 2 stitches, lifted increase in next stitch, k1.

✳ TECHNIQUE ✳

Lifted increases (see Glossary, page 167) are the best increases in stockinette stitch.

Work 7 (7, 5, 3, 3) rows even.

Repeat last 8 (8, 6, 4, 4) rows 10 (12, 12, 17, 19) times more—57 (61, 67, 77, 83) stitches.

Work even until piece measures 18½" (47cm). End after working a WS row.

(Shorten or lengthen for sleeve length here.)

SHAPE SLEEVE CAP

Bind off 4 (5, 6, 7, 8) stitches at beginning of next 2 rows—49 (51, 55, 63, 67) stitches.

Decrease Row (RS) K1, ssk, knit to last 3 stitches, k2tog, k1.

Purl 1 row.

Repeat the last 2 rows 10 (10, 13, 17, 19) times more—27 stitches. End after working a WS row.

Bind off 4 stitches at beginning of next 2 rows, then 2 stitches at beginning of next 2 rows. Bind off remaining stitches.

FINISHING

Sew shoulder seams, adjusting for the different numbers of stitches between the Fronts and Back. Sew in Sleeves.

Sew side and Sleeve seams, adjusting for the different numbers of stitches between the Fronts and Back at underarm bind-offs.

NECK EDGING

With RS facing and beginning at neck edge of Right Front, pick up and knit around entire neck edge as follows:

- 1 stitch for every bound-off stitch
- 1 stitch for every 2-row step between bound-off stitches
- 3 stitches for every 4 rows (along straight edges)
- 1 stitch for every stitch on holder

—approximately 97 (100, 100, 106, 106) stitches.

Over next row, decrease or increase as needed to this number.

WS Rows P1, *k2, p1; repeat from * to end.

RS Rows K1, *p2, k1; repeat from * to end.

Repeat last 2 rows to ½" (13mm), then bind off in pattern.

✳ FLATTER & FIT ✳

You will notice that we never give you a total for the correct number of stitches for the front bands. This is because you may have shortened or lengthened your garment, and so there isn't one right number for every knitter's front band. The proportion and the correct multiple are what you need to know.

BUTTON BAND

With RS facing and beginning at neck edge of Left Front, pick up and knit 3 stitches for every 4 rows along entire Front edge.

Count stitches. Over next row, decrease or increase evenly, as needed, to a multiple of 3 + 1 stitch.

Work 1x2 rib as Neck Edging for 1" (2.5cm), then bind off in pattern.

Mark places in the p2's of the button band for 5 or 6 evenly spaced buttons.

BUTTONHOLE BAND

With RS facing and beginning at lower edge of Right Front, pick up and knit in same manner as button band: in the next row, decrease or increase to same number of stitches as button band.

Work 1x2 rib as neck edging for 2 rows.

Next (WS) Row, Make Buttonholes Work in rib as established to WS k2's that are marked for buttonholes. At these places, work k2 as [k2tog, yo].

Next Row (RS) Work in rib as established, taking care not to twist the yo's.

Continue in rib to 1" (2.5cm), then bind off in pattern.

Sew buttons to button band to match placement of buttonholes.

The Sweater Sally Made Instead

DESIGNED BY SALLY

When Caddy asked me to do a simple rib cardigan, I began as asked. But after only an inch of rib, I thought "She doesn't really want something that simple, does she?" And so I diverted the ribs to cables and baskets and bobbles . . . and produced a sweater she didn't really want (although she gamely wore it anyway).

But really! Wouldn't it have been better for me to do as asked? Yes! Then I could have watched her wear her cardigan through many years of laundry and joyful events. But, on the other hand, I wouldn't have had this story to tell, this lesson to learn, or this pattern to offer.

SKILL LEVEL
Experienced

SIZES
> S (M, L, 1X, 2X)
> Finished bust 34½ (40, 44, 49½, 53)" (87.5 [101.5, 112, 125.5, 134.5]cm)
> Finished length 19 (19½, 20, 20½, 21)" (48.5 [49.5, 51, 52, 53.5]cm)
> Finished shoulder width 15" (38cm)
> Finished sleeve length 29 (29½, 30, 30½, 31)" (74 [75, 76, 77.5, 79]cm)

Model is shown in size M.

MATERIALS
> 1470 (1600, 1800, 1960, 2020)yd (1325 [1470, 1620, 1765, 1910]m) / 11 (12, 14, 15, 16) balls Nashua Cilantro (70% cotton / 30% polyester each approximately 1¾oz [50g] and 136yd [125m]), in color NCIL0022 (lavender gray), (4) medium
> One pair size 6 (4mm) needles
> One pair size 8 (5mm) needles, or size needed to obtain gauge
> Cable needle
> Stitch holder
> Spare needle
> 8 buttons, ⅝" (16mm) wide

INSPIRATION

I found the cable pattern in an old and favorite stitch dictionary. But the basket of buds was something I worked out myself—to run continuously into the cables and to showcase one of my favorite stitches, no-turn bobbles.

✳ FLATTER & FIT ✳

Sleeve length is measured from center body to end of sleeve. For more information, see Glossary, page 167.

GAUGE

> 17 stitches and 26 rows = 4″ (10cm) in stockinette stitch, over larger needles
> 22 stitches and 26 rows = 4″ (10cm) in 3x2 cable, over larger needles

Sweater

RIGHT FRONT + BACK + LEFT FRONT
* TECHNIQUE *

There are no side seams: the fronts and back are knit in one piece to the underarm. (This was done because it was difficult to start and stop the cables at the side seams and over multiple sizes without drawing many different charts.)

EDGING

With smaller needles, cable cast on 182 (210, 234, 262, 286) stitches.

* TECHNIQUE *

I like the cable cast-on (see Glossary, page 167) for this kind of work: its heaviness provides an appropriately decorative edge.

Work 2x2 rib (beginning and ending each RS row with k2 and each WS row with p2) for 6 rows. End after working a WS row.

Sizes S (L, 2X), Next Row Knit, increasing 2 stitches evenly across row—184 (236, 288) stitches.
Sizes M (1X), Next Row Knit.
All Sizes, Next Row (WS) Knit.

BODY

Change to larger needles, and knit 1 more (RS) row.
Set-Up Row for Basket-of-Buds Chart (WS) K5, [p5, k8] to last 10 stitches, p5, k5.
Beginning with row 1 of chart, work baskets-of-buds for 10 rows.
Row 11 (RS) Work chart over 11 stitches, purl into next stitch on left needle but do not remove stitch from left needle, use original stitch on left needle to work cable cross as written; continue row 11 from chart to last 14 stitches; work cable cross as written but end with kf&b into stitch on cn, work to end of row 11 of chart—186 (212, 238, 264, 290) stitches.
Row 12 Work from chart.
Row 13 Work from chart for first 15 stitches; k2,*k9, work cable 4 over next 4 stitches; repeat from * 10

(12, 14, 16, 18) times more, k11; work from chart for last 15 stitches.

Row 14 Work from chart.

Row 15 Work from chart.

Next Row, Row 4 of Basket-of-Buds Chart + Set-Up Row for 3x2 Cable Chart (WS) Work first 14 stitches as row 4 of basket-of-buds; k1, p2, [k3, p5, k6, p5, k3, p4] to last 39 stitches; k3, p5, k6, p5, k3, p2, k1; work last 14 stitches as row 4 of basket-of-buds.

Next Row (RS) Work first 14 stitches as row 5 of basket-of-buds; k1, beginning at right edge of chart, work row 1 of 3x2 cable chart to 26-stitch repeat line; work 26-stitch repeat 4 (5, 6, 7, 8) times; work to left edge of chart and to last 15 stitches, k1; work last 14 stitches as row 5 of basket-of-buds.

Continue working from both charts as follows: begin with row 6 of basket-of-buds and row 2 of 3x2 cable; begin and end all rows with 14 stitches of basket-of-buds and with k1 between the two charts. Work until piece measures 11″ (28cm). End after working a WS row. *Note which chart rows you end with, so when you begin again you can begin on the correct row.*

(Shorten or lengthen for finished length here.)

RIGHT FRONT SHAPE ARMHOLE

Work 1 RS row as established by charts over 47 (54, 61, 68, 75) stitches.

Put remaining 139 (158, 177, 196, 215) stitches onto spare needle.

Work from charts as established through all following rows.

Turn. Bind off 2 (4, 7, 10, 13) stitches, work to end—45 (50, 54, 58, 62) stitches.

Decrease Row (RS) Work to last 4 stitches, work 2 together, k2.

✸ TECHNIQUE ✸

The decrease suggests "work 2 together" rather than k2tog because sometimes the stitch pattern will work out better if you p2tog. (In subsequent pieces you'll choose between skp and p2tog.) P2tog's don't have any particular lean when viewed from the RS, so you may p2tog in all these situations.

Work 1 WS row.

Repeat the last 2 rows 2 (7, 11, 15, 19) times more—42 stitches.

If you make the shoulders to our size, after the final decrease there will be an extra stitch (beyond the charted 26-stitch repeat) at the armhole: work this selvedge stitch as a RS purl and WS knit.

(Widen or narrow for shoulder width by working fewer or more decreases.)

Continue even until armhole measures 5 (5½, 6, 6½, 7)″ (12.5 [14, 15, 16.5, 18]cm). End after working a WS row.

RIGHT FRONT, SHAPE NECK AND SHOULDER

Continuing in pattern, at neck edge bind off 8 stitches once, 3 stitches once, 2 stitches twice, then 1 stitch 7 times—20 stitches remain. AT THE SAME TIME, when armhole measures 7 (7½, 8, 8½, 9)″ (18 [19, 20.5, 21.5, 23]cm), bind off 5 stitches at armhole edge 4 times —0 stitches.

BACK, SHAPE ARMHOLE

Return to remaining 139 (158, 177, 196, 215) stitches, RS facing.

Work from chart as established through all following rows.

Beginning with noted row on chart, bind off 2 (4, 7, 10, 13) stitches, work to 90 (100, 109, 118, 127) stitches on right needle.

Turn. Leave remaining 47 (54, 61, 68, 75) stitches on a spare needle.

Bind off 2 (4, 7, 10, 13) stitches, work to end—88 (96, 102, 108, 114) stitches.

Decrease Row (RS) K2, work 2 together, work in pattern to last 4 stitches, work 2 together, k2.

Work 1 WS row.

Repeat the last 2 rows 3 (7, 10, 13, 16) times more—80 stitches.

If you make the shoulders to our size, after the final decreases, there will be an extra stitch (beyond the charted 26-stitch repeat) at the armholes: work these selvedge stitches as a RS purl and WS knit.

(Widen or narrow for shoulder width as Right Front.)

Continue even until armhole measures same length as Right Front to shoulder shaping. End after working a WS row.

BACK, SHAPE RIGHT SHOULDER AND NECK

Bind off 5 stitches, work to 17 stitches on right needle. Put center 36 stitches on holder for Back neck. Turn.

Bind off 1 stitch at neck edge, work to end. Bind off 5 stitches at armhole edge, work to end. Repeat the last 2 rows once.

On the next RS row, bind off remaining 5 stitches.

BACK, SHAPE LEFT SHOULDER AND NECK

Work 1 RS row over remaining 22 stitches. Bind off 5 stitches at armhole edge.

Work as Right Shoulder and Neck from * to *.
On the next WS row, bind off remaining 5 stitches.

LEFT FRONT, SHAPE ARMHOLE
Return to remaining 47 (54, 61, 68, 75) stitches, RS facing.
Beginning with noted row on chart, bind off 2 (4, 7, 10, 13) stitches, work to end.
Work 1 WS row.
Decrease Row (RS) K2, work 2 together, work to end.
Repeat the last 2 rows 2 (7, 11, 15, 19) times more—42 stitches.
If you make your shoulders to our size, after the final decrease, there will be an extra stitch (beyond the charted 26-stitch repeat) at the armhole: work this selvedge stitch as a RS purl and WS knit.
(Widen or narrow for shoulder width as Right Front.)
Continue until armhole measures same length as Right Front to neck edge. End after working a RS row.

LEFT FRONT, SHAPE NECK AND SHOULDER
Continuing in pattern, at neck edge bind off 8 stitches once, 3 stitches once, 2 stitches twice, then 1 stitch 7 times—20 stitches remain. AT THE SAME TIME, when armhole measures same length as Right Front to

shoulder shaping, bind off 5 stitches at armhole edge 4 times—0 stitches.

SLEEVES
EDGING
With smaller needles, cable cast on 42 (42, 50, 50, 58) stitches.
Work as Back edging.

BODY
Increase Row (RS) K3 (3, 4, 4, 5) *K2 (2, 2, 2, 3), kf&b; repeat from * to last 3 (3, 4, 4, 5) stitches, k3 (3, 4, 4, 5)—54 (54, 64, 64, 70) stitches.
Set-Up Row for 3x2 Cable Chart (WS)
Sizes S & M Only K1, *k3, p5, k3, p4, k3, p5, k3; repeat from * once, k1.
Sizes L (1X) Only K1, p2, k3, *k3, p5, k3, p4, k3, p5, k3; repeat from * once, k3, p2, k1.
Size 2X Only K1, p5, k3, *k3, p5, k3, p4, k3, p5, k3; repeat from * once, k3, p5, k1.
Next Row, All Sizes P1, beginning and ending where noted for size, work row 1 from 3x2 cable chart to last stitch, p1.

The Sweater Sally Made Instead

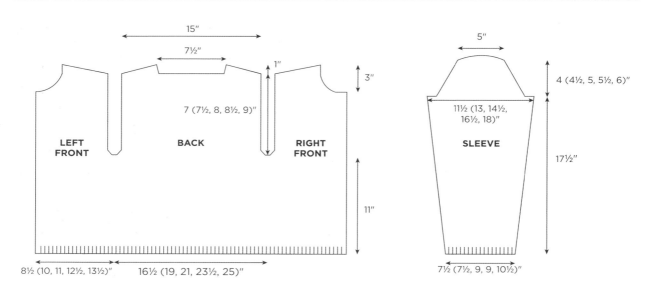

BASKET-OF-BUDS CHART (OVER A MULTIPLE OF 13 + 15 STITCHES)

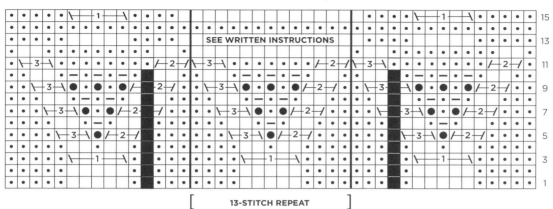

[**13-STITCH REPEAT**]

■ No stitch

□ RS knit, WS purl

• RS purl, WS knit

— slip 1 purlwise

● no-turn bobble (knit cast on 3 stitches onto left needle, p4, pass 2nd, then 3rd, then 4th over 1st — as if binding off)

⌐1⌐ Place 2 stitches from left needle onto cn to front, k2 from left needle, p1 from left needle, k2 from cn

⌐2⌐ Place 1 stitch from left needle onto cn to back, k2 from left needle, p1 from cn

⌐3⌐ Place 2 stitches from left needle onto cn to front, p1 from left needle, k2 from cn

⌐4⌐ Place 2 stitches from left needle onto cn to front, k2 from left needle, k2 from cn (appears in row 13 only)

3X2 CABLE CHART

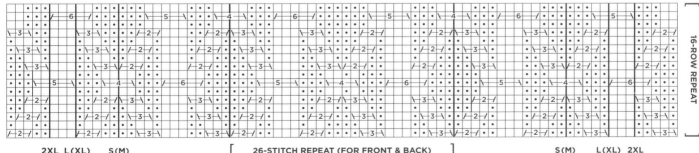

2XL L(XL)   S(M) [**26-STITCH REPEAT (FOR FRONT & BACK)**] **S(M)   L(XL) 2XL**

[Size lines for Sleeves only.] [Size lines for Sleeves only.]

16-ROW REPEAT

□ RS knit, WS purl

• RS purl, WS knit

⌐2⌐ Place 1 stitch from left needle onto cn to back, k2 from left needle, p1 from cn

⌐3⌐ Place 2 stitches from left needle onto cn to front, p1 from left needle, k2 from cn

⌐4⌐ Place 2 stitches from left needle onto cn to front, k2 from left needle, k2 from cn

⌐5⌐ Place 2 stitches from left needle onto cn to front, k3 from left needle, k2 from cn

⌐6⌐ Place 3 stitches from left needle onto cn to back, k2 from left needle, k3 from cn

✳ TECHNIQUE ✳

As you work the increases (that follow) you may work stitches that fall outside the chart in reverse stockinette (as I did), or you may extend the chart. But do not work the cable crosses if all of its stitches are not yet available.

Beginning and ending WS rows with k1 and RS rows with p1, work from chart to 12 (8, 8, 6, 6) rows. End after working a WS row.

Increase Row (RS) P1, work lifted increase in next stitch, work from chart to last 2 stitches, work lifted increase in next stitch, p1.

Work 11 (7, 7, 5, 5) rows even.

Repeat the last 12 (8, 8, 6, 6) rows 4 (8, 7, 12, 13) times more—64 (72, 80, 90, 98) stitches.

Work even until piece measures 17½" (44.5cm). End after working a WS row.

(Shorten or lengthen for sleeve length here.)

CAP

Bind off 3 (5, 8, 11, 14) stitches at the beginning of the next 2 rows—58 (62, 64, 68, 70) stitches.

✳ TECHNIQUE ✳

There is one more stitch bound off for the sleeves than for the front and back because this extra stitch will be taken into the sleeve's seam allowance.

Decrease Row (RS) K2, skp, work in pattern to last 4 stitches, k2tog, k2.

Work 1 WS row.

Repeat the last 2 rows 14 (16, 17, 19, 20) times more—28 stitches. End after working the RS row that results in 28 stitches.

Bind off 2 stitches at the beginning of the next 2 rows, then 4 stitches at the beginning of the next 2 rows. Bind off remaining 16 stitches.

FINISHING

NECK EDGING

Sew shoulder seams.

With smaller needle, pick up and knit as follows:

- 1 stitch for every bound-off stitch
- 1 stitch for every 2-row step between bound-off stitches
- 3 stitches for every 4 rows (along straight edges)
- 1 stitch for every stitch on holder

—approximately 117 stitches.

Decrease Row (WS) *K3, skp, repeat from * to last 2

stitches—approximately 94 stitches.

**Next Row Knit, increasing or decreasing evenly, and as needed, to a multiple of 4 + 2 stitches.

Work 2x2 rib (beginning and ending RS rows with k2 and WS rows with p2) for 5 rows, then bind off in rib.

BUTTON BAND

With smaller needles and RS facing, pick up and knit 3 stitches for every 4 rows along Left Front.

Knit 1 row.

Work as for Neck Edging from ** to end.

BUTTONHOLE BAND

Mark places in RS p2's of button band for 8 evenly spaced buttonholes.

With smaller needles and RS facing, pick up and knit 3 stitches for every 4 rows along Right Front.

Knit 1 row.

Next Row Knit, increasing or decreasing evenly, and as needed, to same number of stitches as button band.

Work 2x2 rib as Neck Edging for 1 row.

✳ TECHNIQUE ✳

The 3-row buttonhole that follows is the eyelet buttonhole made a little larger and with reinforcement. If you think the buttonhole is big enough after the eyelet—after row 2—don't work the third row.

Next Row (RS), Begin Buttonholes Work rib as established to places for buttonholes, ending after working k2s; [p2tog, yo] each buttonhole.

Next Row, Continue Buttonholes Work rib as established, knitting yo's to not twist them.

Next Row, Finish Buttonholes Work rib as established to each buttonhole, purl through buttonhole itself, then drop purl stitch from left needle.

Work 2x2 rib for 1 more row, then bind off in pattern.

Sew buttons to button band to match placement of buttonholes.

Sew Sleeves into armholes.

Sew Sleeve seams.

Baby Doll Dress and Petticoat

DESIGNED BY SALLY

This piece expresses the timelessness that I think makes an "heirloom-quality" garment. But although I call it a dress, I think that—for most of us—it's actually the more versatile tunic length. Therefore, it can be worn over pants or a skirt. (And speaking of a skirt, check out the following petticoat pattern: these two pieces were made to be worn together.)

Dress

SKILL LEVEL
Intermediate

SIZES
> S (M, L, 1X, 2X)
> Finished hem 52 (55½, 59½, 63, 67)" (132 [141, 151, 160, 170]cm)
> Finished bust 35 (39, 42½, 46½, 50½)" (89 [99, 108, 118, 128.5]cm)
> Finished shoulder width 14 (14, 16, 16, 16)" (35.5 [35.5, 40.5, 40.5, 40.5]cm)
> Finished length 31½ (32, 32½, 33, 33½)" (80 [81, 82.5, 84, 85]cm)
> Finished sleeve length 28½ (29, 29½, 30, 30½)" 72 [74, 75, 76, 77.5]cm)

Model is shown in size M.

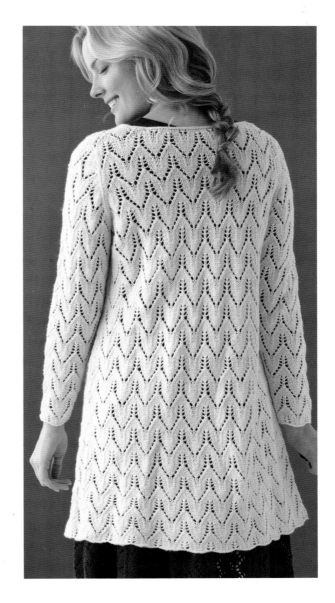

INSPIRATION

This piece was modeled after a favorite top that I own and wear. Often enough, my inspiration comes from my closet!

MATERIALS

> 1500 (1675, 1850, 2010, 2180)yd (1350 [1500, 1665, 1810, 1960]m) / 8 (9, 10, 11, 12) balls Rowan Classic Cashsoft 4ply (57% merino, 33% acrylic, 10% cashmere, each approximately 1¾oz [50g] and 197yd [180m]), in color 433 (cream), (2) fine
> One pair size 5 (3.75mm) needles, or size needed to obtain gauge
> One pair size 3 (3.25mm) needles
> 2 stitch holders
> 2 stitch markers

GAUGE

21 stitches and 30 rows = 4" (10cm) in stitch pattern, over larger needles and after steam-pressing

PATTERN NOTE

Lace tends to open up, so this garment could stretch up to 2" (5cm) with washing and wearing.

STITCH PATTERN

(over a multiple of 10 + 1 stitch)
Rows 1, 3, 5 *K1, skp, k2, yo, k1, yo, k2, k2tog; repeat from * to last stitch, k1.

All WS Rows Purl.
Row 7 *K1, yo, skp, k5, k2tog, yo; repeat from * to last stitch, k1.
Row 9 *K2, yo, skp, k3, k2tog, yo, k1; repeat from * to last stitch, k1.
Row 11 *K3, yo, skp, k1, k2tog, yo, k2; repeat from * to last stitch, k1.
Row 13 *K4, yo, s2kp, yo, k3; repeat from * to last stitch, k1.

BACK

With larger needles, long-tail cast on 123 (133, 143, 153, 163) stitches.
Purl 1 row.
Next Row (RS) K1, work row 1 of stitch pattern (from written directions or from chart) to last stitch, k1.
Row 2 P1, work row 2 to last stitch, p1.
Continue as established—in stitch pattern but with 1 stockinette stitch at each edge—to 8 rows.

SHAPE SIDES

Decrease Row (RS) K1, skp, work stitch pattern as established to last 3 stitches, k2tog, k1.

✳ TECHNIQUE ✳
When working lace that is shaped, be careful to maintain the lace pattern through decreases or increases. If there are not enough stitches to work the decrease that pairs with a yo, do not work the yo, and vice versa. Extra stitches as the edges are just worked in stockinette stitch.

Work 9 rows even.
(Shorten or lengthen for finished length by working fewer or more rows between side decreases. But do end with the indicated number of rows for armhole shaping.)
Repeat the last 10 rows 14 times more—93 (103, 113, 123, 133) stitches.
Work even until piece measures 24" (61cm) (or your desired length). End after working a WS row.

SHAPE ARMHOLE

Bind off 3 (5, 7, 9, 11) stitches at beginning of next 2 rows—87 (93, 99, 105, 111) stitches.
Decrease Row (RS) K1, skp, work to last 3 stitches, k2tog, k1.
Work 1 row even.
Repeat the last 2 rows 6 (9, 7, 10, 13) times more—73 (73, 83, 83, 83) stitches.

✳ FLATTER & FIT ✳

The armhole is shallow for this garment because it suits the style, *and* a narrower upper sleeve makes us look slimmer. If you wish deeper armholes (and wider sleeves), work to the armhole depth of a larger size, and then work that larger size sleeve.

(Widen or narrow for shoulder width by working fewer or more decreases.)

Work even until armhole measures 6½ (7, 7½, 8, 8½)" (16.5 [18, 19, 20.5, 21.5]cm). End after working a WS row.

SHAPE RIGHT SHOULDER AND BACK NECK

Work to 19 (19, 24, 24, 24) stitches on right needle. Put center 35 stitches onto holder. Turn.
*Bind off 2 stitches at neck edge, work to end.
Bind off 5 stitches at armhole edge, work to end.
Repeat from * once.

Work neck edge even while binding off 5 stitches at armhole edge 1 (1, 2, 2, 2) more time(s)—0 stitches.

SHAPE LEFT SHOULDER AND BACK NECK

Beginning with a RS row, work 2 rows over remaining 19 (19, 24, 24, 24) stitches.
Work as Shape Right Shoulder and Back Neck from * to end.

FRONT

With larger needles, long-tail cast on 153 (163, 173, 183, 193) stitches.
Purl 1 row.
Work as Back to end of Shape Sides—123 (133, 143, 153, 163) stitches.
Work even until piece measures 2″ (5cm) shorter than Back to armhole. End after working a WS row.

GATHER NECK

Continuing in stitch pattern as established, work to 26 (31, 36, 41, 46) stitches on right needle, place marker, *slip 1 purlwise, k4; repeat from * 13 times more, slip 1 purlwise, place marker—71 stitches in neck—work to end in stitch pattern as established.

✳ TECHNIQUE ✳

Always slip knitwise or purlwise as directed by the pattern. But never move the yarn from where it already is unless directed by the pattern. Patterns that need you to move it read "wyif" or "wyib." This pattern does not, because you want to leave the yarn where it already is—in the back for a knit row, in the front for a purl row. (See Glossary, page 167.)

All following directions for slip 1 purlwise will read "sl 1."
Next Row Purl.
Repeat the last 2 rows once more.
Neck Decrease Row (RS) Work stitches outside markers as established, work stitches inside marker as follows: *sl 1, [k2tog] twice; repeat from * to last stitch before marker, sl 1—43 stitches between markers, 95 (105, 115, 125, 135) stitches in row.
Next Row (WS) Purl.
Next Row (RS) Work stitches outside markers as established, work stitches inside marker as follows: *sl 1, k2; repeat from * to last stitch before marker, sl 1. Repeat the last 2 rows until piece measures same length as Back to armhole. End after working a WS row.

SHAPE ARMHOLE AND FINISH NECK

Bind off 3 (5, 7, 9, 11) stitches at beginning of next 2 rows—89 (95, 101, 107, 113) stitches.

Decrease Row (RS) K1, skp, work as established (through lace and across neck) to last 3 stitches, k2tog, k1.

Work 1 WS row.

Repeat the last 2 rows 2 (2, 4, 6, 8) times more—83 (89, 91, 93, 95) stitches.

Decrease Row and Finish Neck (RS) K1, skp, work as established to marker, bind off center 43 stitches, remove markers, work to last 3 stitches, k2tog, k1. Put 19 (22, 23, 24, 25) stitches of Left Front onto holder.

SHAPE RIGHT ARMHOLE AND SHOULDER

Purl 1 row (over remaining stitches of Right Front).

Decrease Row (RS) Work stitch pattern to last 3 stitches, k2tog, k1.

Work 1 WS row.

Repeat the last 2 rows 3 (6, 2, 3, 4) times more—15 (15, 20, 20, 20) stitches.

(Widen or narrow for shoulder width as for Back.) Work even until armhole measures same length as Back to shoulder shaping. End after working a RS row. Bind off 5 stitches at beginning of next 3 (3, 4, 4, 4) WS rows—0 stitches.

SHAPE LEFT ARMHOLE AND SHOULDER

Return to remaining 19 (22, 23, 24, 25) stitches, WS facing.

Purl 1 row.

Decrease Row (RS) K1, skp, work to end.

Work 1 WS row.

Repeat the last 2 rows 3 (6, 2, 3, 4) times more—15 (15, 20, 20, 20) stitches.

(Widen or narrow for shoulder width as for Back.) Work even until armhole measures same length as Back to shoulder shaping. End after working a WS row. Bind off 5 stitches at beginning of next 3 (3, 4, 4, 4) RS rows—0 stitches.

SLEEVES

With larger needles, long-tail cast on 43 (43, 53, 53, 53) stitches.

Purl 1 row.

Next Row (RS) K1, work row 1 of stitch pattern from written directions or from chart to last stitch, k1.

Row 2 P1, work row 2 to last stitch, p1.

Continue as established—in stitch pattern but with 1 stockinette stitch at each edge—to 8 rows.

Increase Row K1, work lifted increase in next stitch, work stitch pattern to last 2 stitches, work lifted increase in next stitch, k1.

Baby Doll Dress

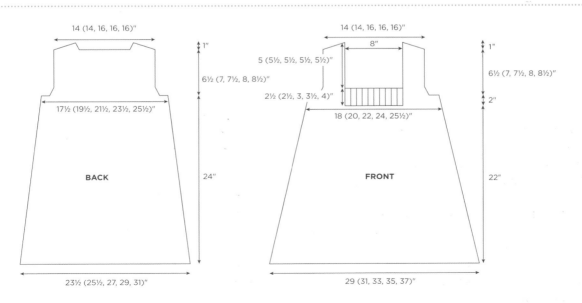

Work 7 (5, 5, 5, 3) rows even.

Repeat Increase Row.

Work 7 (7, 7, 5, 5) rows even.

Repeat the last 16 (14, 14, 12, 10) rows 6 (7, 7, 9, 11) times more—71 (75, 85, 93, 101) stitches.

Work even until pieces measures 17 (17, 16, 16, 16)" (43 [43, 40.5, 40.5, 40.5]cm). End after working a WS row. (Shorten or lengthen for sleeve length here.)

SHAPE SLEEVE CAP

Bind off 3 (5, 7, 9, 11) stitches at beginning of next 2 rows—65 (65, 71, 75, 79) stitches.

Decrease Row (RS) K1, skp, work to last 3 stitches, k2tog, k1.

Work 1 WS row.

Repeat the last 2 rows 17 (17, 20, 22, 24) times more—29 stitches.

Bind off 2 stitches at beginning of next 2 rows.

Bind off 4 stitches at beginning of next 2 rows.

Bind off 17 stitches.

FINISHING

Steam-press all pieces.

Sew shoulder seams.

Sew Sleeves into armholes.

To make the Sleeve fit, ease in the extra fabric at the cap. This is a very slightly puffed sleeve.

Sew side and Sleeve seams.

NECK EDGING

With smaller needle and RS facing, begin at corner of Right Front neck edge (at end of neck bind-off) and end at corner of Left Front neck edge (at beginning of neck bind-off) to pick up and knit as follows:

- 3 stitches for every 4 rows (along straight edges)
- 1 stitch for every bound-off stitch
- 1 stitch for every 2-row step between bound-off stitches
- 1 stitch for every stitch on holder

—approximately 132 stitches.

You are not picking up along the front neck, bound-off edge.

Knit 1 row, purl 1 row, then bind off knitwise.

Sew corners of neck edging down.

Baby Doll Dress

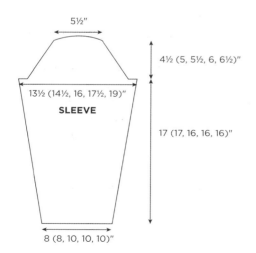

5½"

4½ (5, 5½, 6, 6½)"

13½ (14½, 16, 17½, 19)"

SLEEVE

17 (17, 16, 16, 16)"

8 (8, 10, 10, 10)"

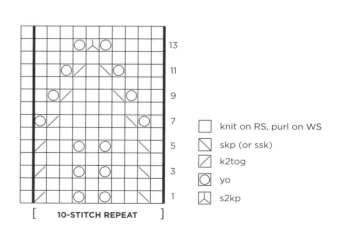

	knit on RS, purl on WS
	skp (or ssk)
	k2tog
	yo
	s2kp

13   11   9   7   5   3   1

[**10-STITCH REPEAT**   ]

Petticoat

SKILL LEVEL
Intermediate

SIZE
One size
All measurements are approximate.
> Finished circumference 72" (183cm)
> Height (not including slip) 6½" (16.5cm)

MATERIALS
> See Pattern Notes for additional information about yarn amounts and colors.
> 300yd (273m) / 2 balls Rowan Classic Cashsoft 4ply (57% merino, 33% acrylic, 10% cashmere, each approximately 1¾oz [50g] and 197yd [180m]), in color 432 (brown), ② fine
> One pair size 5 (3.75mm) needles
> One black slip, 6½" (16.5cm) shorter than your desired finished length
> Embroidery needle (or sharp tapestry needle)

GAUGE
Approximately 21 stitches and 30 rows = 4" (10cm) in lace, after steam-pressing.
Gauge does not matter.

PATTERN NOTES
1. The length of the petticoat (and the amount of yarn required) is based upon your attaching the petticoat to a slip 6½" (16.5cm) shorter than the length you want. If your slip is shorter than this—and you need to give the petticoat more length—your yarn amount will increase.
2. I have shortened slips by just cutting them with scissors. They don't seem to suffer from this, although you want to be sure to cut a straight line!
3. If you make a light-colored petticoat, attach it to a light-colored slip; if you make a dark-colored petticoat (as I did), attach it to a dark-colored slip.
4. The pattern calls for 3 panels that are sewn together to form the circumference.
5. To see the petticoat alone, go to www.sallymelvilleknits.com and click on "Books."

PANELS (MAKE 3)
Long-tail cast on 123 stitches.
Purl 1 row.
Following Rows Beginning with row 1, work from chart or with following written directions.

INSPIRATION

I once wore the Baby Doll Dress with a skirt but lamented that the skirt was not lace. So then I thought, "Why not knit a lace skirt?" Ah yes, but when worn with the Baby Doll Dress we're only going to see the lower bit of it. So why not knit *only* the portion that will be seen? Attaching it to a slip was the answer, and the result is this petticoat, meant to be worn with the Baby Doll Dress or with any of your favorite tunics.

Row 1 K1, k2tog, k4, yo, *k1, yo, k4, s2kp, k4, yo; repeat from * to last 8 stitches, k1, yo, k4, skp, k1.

All WS Rows Purl.

Row 3 K1, k2tog, k3, yo, k1, *k2, yo, k3, s2kp, k3, yo, k1; repeat from * to last 8 stitches, k2, yo, k3, skp, k1.

Row 5 K1, k2tog, k2, yo, k2, *k3, yo, k2, s2kp, k2, yo, k2; repeat from * to last 8 stitches, k3, yo, k2, skp, k1.

Row 7 K1, k2tog, [k1, yo] twice, skp, *k1, k2tog, [yo, k1] twice, s2kp, [k1, yo] twice, skp; repeat from * to last 8 stitches, k1, k2tog, [yo, k1] twice, skp, k1.

Row 9 K1, k2tog, yo, k3, yo, *s2kp, yo, k3, yo, s2kp, yo, k3, yo; repeat from * to last 8 stitches, s2kp, yo, k3, yo, skp, k1.

Work until piece measures 6″ (15cm). End after working a WS row.

(Shorten or lengthen here so the panels plus the slip give the length needed.)

Bind off.

FINISHING

Steam-press pieces.

Sew the three lace panels together so the k1 at the edge of one piece overlaps the k1 at the edge of the adjoining piece.

This method of sewing will allow the k1 at one edge to look like the center stitch that defines a panel.

Around entire hem of slip, and with some remaining yarn, embroider a running stitch, or a blanket stitch, or any embroidered stitch you know, spacing stitches as evenly as possible.

Before attaching the lace to the slip, use a calculator to determine your ratio (as follows). Then use some remaining yarn to sew the lace to the slip as indicated below.

- Count the number of stitches you embroidered around the hem of the slip
- Divide the number of stitches you embroidered by 366 (the number of stitches in the lace)
- If your ratio is .333, sew 1 embroidered stitch to every 3 bound-off stitches
- If your ratio is .4, sew 2 embroidered stitches to every 5 bound-off stitches
- If your ratio is .5, sew 1 embroidered stitch to every 2 bound-off stitches
- If your ratio is .6, sew 3 embroidered stitches to every 5 bound-off stitches
- If your ratio is .67, sew 2 embroidered stitches to every 3 bound-off stitches
- If your ratio is .75, sew 3 embroidered stitches to every 4 bound-off stitches
- If your ratio is between these numbers, fudge!

It doesn't need to be sewn perfectly evenly; remember that the knitting is gathered.

Petticoat

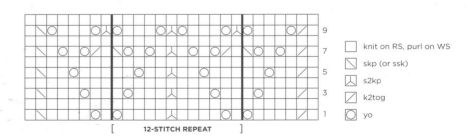

12-STITCH REPEAT

	knit on RS, purl on WS
⟍	skp (or ssk)
⅄	s2kp
⟋	k2tog
○	yo

ONE (OF THREE) PANELS

6½″

24″

Groovy Pullover

DESIGNED BY SALLY

I would love to be able to say where the inspiration for this stitch pattern came from—perhaps from a counterpane afghan? The place of departure remains dimly lit in my brain. What I do remember is knitting a swatch—starting with the wavy ridge, which produced a kind of scalloped lower edge—and thinking "The guys won't like *that*!" And so I worked out how to "fill" it. It was fun for me to figure it out, and I hope you have as much fun knitting it.

SKILL LEVEL
Experienced

SIZES
> S (M, L, 1X, 2X)
> Finished chest 41 (45, 49, 53, 57)" (104 [114.5, 124.5, 134.5, 144.5]cm)
> Finished length 25½ (26, 26½, 27, 27½)" (65 [66, 67.5, 68.5, 70]cm)
> Finished sleeve length 31 (32, 33, 34, 35)" (78.5 [81, 84, 86.5, 89]cm)

Model is shown in size S.

MATERIALS
> 1885 (2075, 2260, 2450, 2640)yd (1700 [1865, 2035, 2205, 2375]m) / 19 (21, 22, 24, 26) balls Rowan Denim (100% cotton, each approximately 1¾oz [50g] and 102yd [93m]), in color 225 (Nashville), (3) light
> One circular needle, size 5 (3.75mm), 20" (51cm), or size needed to obtain gauge
> 16 stitch markers
> 2 stitch holders

GAUGE
> 20 stitches and 34 rows = 4" (10cm) in straight ridge stitch pattern, before washing Rowan Denim
> 22 stitches and 34 rows = 4" (10cm) in straight ridge stitch pattern, after washing Rowan Denim, after pressing any other yarn
> 27 stitches and 34 rows = 4" (10cm) in wavy ridge stitch pattern, after washing Rowan Denim, after pressing any other yarn

STITCH PATTERNS

Straight Ridge Pattern
Rows 1 and 2 Knit.
Rows 3 and 4 Purl.

Wavy Ridge Pattern
(over a multiple of 30 stitches between markers, and over 4 rows)
This stitch pattern, used for most of the garment, is complex and written out within the body and sleeves, when it is used.

PATTERN NOTES

1. Even though the Rowan Denim's label suggests it is a weight 4, because it shrinks in width its final gauge is a weight 3. Therefore, a weight 3 designation is appropriate, and you will get the best results if you substitute with a weight 3.
2. The circular needle is required for the neck edging, the garment itself is knit on the circular or straights.
3. While the gauge is given over the wavy ridge pattern, it is difficult to measure. Making a swatch over the straight ridge pattern will ensure accuracy.
4. The wavy ridge pattern is worked over a center multiple of 30 stitches: stitches at the edges (for larger sizes) are worked in the straight ridge pattern. The pattern makes this clear.

Pullover

FRONT/BACK (MAKE 2)
The front and back are identical; neck shaping occurs in the saddle.

EDGING
Long-tail cast on 115 (126, 137, 148, 159) stitches.
Knit 1 row, then purl 1 row.
Increase Row (WS) [P8, increase 1 in next stitch) 12 (13, 14, 15, 16) times, end with k7 (9, 11, 13, 15)—127 (139, 151, 163, 175) stitches.

LOWER RIGHT EDGE SHORT ROWS
Short Row 1 (RS) K16 (22, 28, 34, 40). Turn.
Row 2 Sl 1, k15 (21, 27, 33, 39).
Slip all stitches purlwise and with yarn on WS.
Short Row 3 P14 (20, 26, 32, 38). Turn.
Row 4 Sl 1, p13 (19, 25, 31, 37).
Short Row 5 K12 (18, 24, 30, 36). Turn.
Row 6 Sl 1, k11 (17, 23, 29, 35).
Continue straight ridge pattern, with slip stitch at beginning of WS rows and leaving 2 stitches behind at end of all RS short rows.
Row 12 (WS) Sl 1, p5 (11, 17, 23, 29).
Cut yarn, leaving an 8″ (20.5cm) tail (to close holes).

LOWER CENTER SECTION SHORT ROWS
With RS facing, slip to 21 (27, 33, 39, 45) stitches on right needle.
*Leaving an 8″ (20.5cm) tail, re-join yarn, and continue with straight ridge pattern as follows.
Short Row 1 (RS) Sl 1, k24. Turn.
Short Row 2 Sl 1, k22. Turn.
Short Row 3 Sl 1, p22. Turn.
Short Row 4 Sl 1, p20. Turn.
Short Row 5 Sl 1, k18. Turn.
Short Row 6 Sl 1, k16. Turn.
Continue in straight ridge pattern, with slip stitches and leaving 2 stitches behind at end of all short rows.
Row 12 (WS) Sl 1, p4.
Cut yarn, leaving an 8″ (20.5cm) tail.
With RS facing, slip 20 stitches from left needle onto right needle.
Repeat from * twice more—16 (22, 28, 34, 40) stitches remain on left needle.

LOWER LEFT EDGE SHORT ROWS
Row 1 (RS) Sl 1, k15 (21, 27, 33, 39).
Short Row *2* K16 (22, 28, 34, 40). Turn.
Row 3 Sl 1, p15 (21, 27, 33, 39).

Short Row 4 P14 (20, 26, 32, 38). Turn.

Row 5 Sl 1, k13 (19, 25, 31, 37).

Short Row 6 K12 (18, 24, 30, 36). Turn.

Continue in straight ridge pattern, with slip stitch at beginning of all RS rows and leaving 2 stitches behind at end of all WS short rows.

Row 12 (WS) P6 (12, 18, 24, 30).

Cut yarn, leaving an 8" (20.5cm) tail.

Slip all stitches onto left needle, ready to work a RS row—127 (139, 151, 163, 175) stitches.

WAVY RIDGE BODY

Begin wavy ridge pattern as follows.

Front/Back, Rows 1 and 2 K1 (7, 13, 19, 25), place marker (pm), *k5, pm, yo, k8, k2tog, pm, k5, pm, skp, k8, yo, pm; repeat from * 3 times more and to last 6 (12, 18, 24, 30) stitches, pm, k6 (12, 18, 24, 30).

✳ TECHNIQUE ✳

Work all yo's on the following row so as to twist them (or you'll get holes). This means that you will work through the non-leading edge—the edge of the stitch not closest to the tip of the needle. You will see a little "x" below the stitch as you twist it.

Rows 3 and 4 Purl.

Continue with wavy ridge stitch pattern (with extra stitches at each side) until piece measures 22 (22½, 23, 23½, 24)" (56 [57, 58.5, 59.5, 61]cm).

End after working row 3.

(Shorten or lengthen for finished length here.)

TOP EDGE SHORT ROWS

Work straight ridge stitch pattern from here to end. Remove markers as you encounter them.

Next (WS) Row Bind off 6 (12, 18, 24, 30) stitches purlwise, purl to 17 stitches on right needle. Turn.

Short Row 1 Sl 1, k7. Turn.

Short Row 2 Sl 1, k9. Turn.

Short Row 3 Sl 1, p11. Turn.

Short Row 4 Sl 1, p13. Turn.

Short Row 5 Sl 1, k15. Turn.

Short Row 6 Sl 1, k17. Turn.

Short Row 7 Sl 1, p22. Turn.

Short Row 8 (WS) Sl 1, bind off 30 stitches (purlwise), purl to 17 stitches on right needle (2 stitches past marker). Turn.

Repeat these 8 rows 3 times more, working the final row 8 as follows: sl 1, bind off 31 (37, 43, 49, 55) stitches (purlwise).

LEFT SLEEVE

EDGING

Long-tail cast on 45 (49, 52, 56, 60) stitches.

K 1 row, then p 1 row.

Increase Row (WS) [P9, increase 1 in next stitch] 4 (4, 5, 5, 5) times, end p5 (9, 2, 6, 10)—49 (53, 57, 61, 65) stitches.

LOWER RIGHT EDGE SHORT ROWS

Short Row 1 (RS) K22 (24, 26, 28, 30). Turn.

Row 2 Sl 1, k21 (23, 25, 27, 29).

Short Row 3 P20 (22, 24, 26, 28). Turn.

Row 4 Sl 1, p19 (21, 23, 25, 27).

Continue in straight ridge pattern, with slip stitch at beginning of all WS rows and leaving 2 stitches behind at end of all RS short rows.

Row 12 (WS) Sl 1, p11 (13, 15, 17, 19).

Cut yarn, leaving an 8″ (20.5cm) tail (to close holes).

LOWER LEFT EDGE SHORT ROWS

With RS facing, slip to 27 (29, 31, 33, 35) stitches on right needle.

Leaving an 8″ (20.5cm) tail, re-join yarn, and continue with straight ridge pattern.

Row 1 (RS) Sl 1, k21 (23, 25, 27, 29).

Short Row 2 K22 (24, 26, 28, 30). Turn.

Row 3 Sl 1, p21 (23, 25, 27, 29).

Short Row 4 P20 (22, 24, 26, 28). Turn.

Continue in straight ridge pattern, with slip stitch at beginning of all RS rows and leaving 2 stitches behind at end of all WS short rows.

Row 12 (WS) Sl 1, p11 (13, 15, 17, 19).

Cut yarn, leaving an 8″ (20.5cm) tail.

Slip all stitches onto left needle, ready to work a RS row—49 (53, 57, 61, 65) stitches.

WAVY RIDGE BODY

Begin wavy ridge pattern as follows.

Rows 1 and 2 K7 (9, 11, 13, 15), pm, k5, pm, yo, k8, k2tog, pm, k5, pm, skp, k8, yo, pm, k12 (14, 16, 18, 20).

Groovy Pullover

FRONT / BACK

22 (22½, 23, 23½, 24)″

21 (23, 25, 27, 29)″

6″

3½″

7 (8, 9, 10, 11)″

18 (18¾, 20, 21½, 23)″

LEFT SLEEVE

20″

8 (9, 9½, 10, 11)″

Rows 3 and 4 Purl.

Continue in wavy ridge pattern as established while shaping Sleeve as follows.

Increase Row K1, increase 1 in next stitch, work to last 2 stitches, increase 1 in next stitch, k1.

Work 3 rows even and in pattern.

Repeat the last 4 rows 24 (24, 26, 28, 30) times more—99 (103, 111, 119, 127) stitches.

Work wavy ridge pattern only over 30 stitches between markers, and work all other stitches in straight ridge pattern (as established).

Work until piece measures 20" (51cm). End after working row 2.

(Shorten or lengthen for sleeve length here.)

SADDLE

Bind off 31 (33, 37, 41, 45) stitches at beginning and end of next 2 rows—37 stitches.

Work wavy ridge pattern as follows.

Rows 1 and 2 K1, pm, k5, pm, yo, k8, k2tog, pm, k5, pm, skp, k8, yo, pm, k6.

Rows 3 and 4 Purl.

Continue wavy ridge stitch pattern until saddle measures 7 (8, 9, 10, 11)" (17.5 [20.5, 23, 25.5, 28]cm). End after working row 3.

Remove markers as you encounter them over the next sections.

Next Row (WS) P23. Turn.

Short Row 1 Sl 1, k7. Turn.

Short Row 2 Sl 1, k9. Turn.

Short Row 3 Sl 1, p11. Turn.

Short Row 4 Sl 1, p13. Turn.

Short Row 5 Sl 1, k15. Turn.

Short Row 6 Sl 1, k17. Turn.

Short Row 7 Sl 1, p22. Turn.

Short Row 8 (WS) Sl 1, p30. Turn.

SHAPE BACK NECK

Work straight ridge stitch pattern from here to end.

Next Row (RS) K19. Turn.

*Shape Back neck by binding off 1 stitch at neck edge 3 times.

Work remaining 16 stitches until Back neck measures 3½" (9cm). End after working a row 4.

Put stitches onto holder.

SHAPE FRONT NECK

Return to remaining 18 stitches, RS facing.

*Continuing with straight ridge pattern, shape Front neck by binding off 5 stitches once, 3 stitches once, 2 stitches twice, 1 stitch 3 times, then bind off remaining 3 stitches.

RIGHT SLEEVE

Work as Left Sleeve to Shape Back Neck.

SHAPE FRONT NECK

Work straight ridge pattern from here to end.

Next Row (RS) K18. Turn.

Work as Left Sleeve, Shape Front Neck, from * to end.

SHAPE BACK NECK

Return to remaining 19 stitches, RS facing.

Work as Left Sleeve, Shape Back Neck from * to end.

FINISHING

Use tails to close any holes in short-row sections.

Sew Sleeve saddles to Front/Back as follows.

- Match upper right corner of Back to corner of Right Sleeve
- Sew Right Sleeve saddle across bound-off stitches of Back to center (adding or subtracting rows of saddle as needed)
- Match upper left corner of Back to corner of Left Sleeve
- Sew Left Sleeve saddle across bound-off stitches of Back to center (adding or subtracting rows of saddle as needed)
- Graft saddle centers together at center Back
- Sew Sleeve bound-off edges to sides of Back.

Sew Sleeves to Front in same manner.

Sew Sleeve and side seams.

NECK EDGING

With circular needle, begin at center Back to pick up and knit around neck edge as follows.

- 3 stitches for every 4 rows (along straight edges)
- 1 stitch for every bound-off stitch
- 1 stitch for every 2-row step between bound-off stitches

—approximately 115 stitches.

Turn. Working in the round, knit 3 rounds, then bind off.

CHAPTER THREE

Keeping Warm

Believe it or not, there are people who believe we must sacrifice
warmth for fashion . . . or fashion for warmth. If you are one, this chapter
should change your mind. (And of course, this chapter is
also for those who simply want to continue being their fashionable selves
during freezing temperatures.)

Not only will you find patterns for garments that will keep you warm through even the coldest of winters, but we've also thrown in some garments for those of us who are cold when inside. (I still can't figure out the mystery behind my body's response to a thermostat setting that I find quite warm in the summer but barely keeps me from shivering during the winter.) And don't pass these garments off as strictly winter knitting either. I know a lot of people who work in office buildings where the air conditioning is turned so high they need warm layers in the summer!

It's amazing what an extra layer over the core can do, and the Cardilero couldn't be a more attractive core-warmer. Wear it over a dress at a formal event or over a blouse or turtleneck at the office.

Sometimes all we need is a light layer on the extremities. I wear my Armwarmers all spring, all fall, and inside in the winter, but then I throw mittens over top when I go out into the real cold. And my brother wears his Fingerless Gloves because he is a musician and needs his fingers free while keeping his hands warm.

And this chapter isn't just about warmth! From the Peaked Cap to the Add-On Afghan, these garments all make great gifts. So for those on your list who are guilty of sacrificing warmth for fashion, or vice versa, you can be the one to save them from either frostbite or being nominated for *What Not to Wear*.

So no more sacrifices! Knit and be fashionably warm.　　　　—CADDY

Simple Felted Scarf

DESIGNED BY CADDY

This project is exactly that—simple. It's a great beginner project that doesn't look at all beginner when done. People will think you're *brilliant!* Because of the nature of the stitch pattern, there are no buttonholes. A button can easily be forced through at any point. And because you can button this scarf anywhere, try wearing it with the ends tucked right up around your neck for extra warmth.

SKILL LEVEL
Easy

SIZES
> One size
All measurements are approximate.
> Finished length (before felting) 32½" (82.5cm)
> Finished width (before felting) 9" (23cm)
> Finished length (after felting) 30" (76cm)
> Finished width (after felting) 6½" (16.5cm)

MATERIALS
> 197yd (180m) / 1 skein Cascade Yarns Soft Spun (100% Peruvian highland wool, each approximately 3½ oz [100g] and 197yd [180m]), in color 2808 (natural), (4) medium
> One pair size 10¾ (7mm) needles
> One button, ½" (13mm) wide

GAUGE
Approximately 16 stitches and 24 rows = 4" (10cm) in stitch pattern, before felting
Gauge does not matter.

Scarf

Cast on 36 stitches.
RS Rows P1 *yo, p2tog; repeat from * to last stitch, p1.
WS Rows Purl.

✳ TECHNIQUE ✳

If you worked all rows as RS rows, you would be working a stitch pattern called "purse stitch," and the piece would hang straight. But because of the WS purl rows, it is an "oblique" stitch pattern that will skew. This is an intentional part of the design that makes it easier to knit and with a more interesting shape to wear.

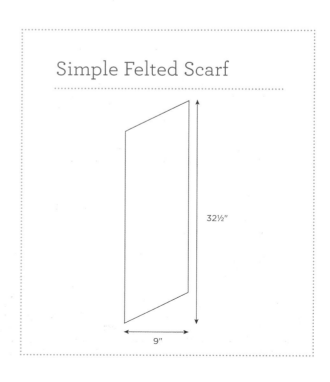

Simple Felted Scarf

32½"

9"

Work stitch pattern until you have only enough yarn to bind off (about 1yd [91cm]). Scarf measures approximately 32½" (82.5cm).
Bind off.

FINISHING
Sew in tails.

✳ TECHNIQUE ✳
Always sew in tails before felting your piece. Otherwise they may become matted messes.

Felt scarf by putting it through one regular warm wash cycle in washing machine. Tumble in dryer on regular heat until dry.

Wrap scarf around your neck, and mark spot for button: the tip of the scarf will overlap across the front up to 6" (15cm).

If your piece feels too big, put it through another wash and dry cycle.

Attach button, and force button through fabric to create buttonhole.

Arm Warmers

DESIGNED BY CADDY

There's something about wearing these arm warmers that makes me feel so stylish. It's probably because they're completely practical and totally cute at the same time. I think they look amazing with a tank top and can definitely be worn in the summer as well as the winter.

SKILL LEVEL
Easy

SIZES

> XS (S-M, L, 1X-2X)
> Finished circumference (at hand) 5 (5¼, 5¼, 5¾)" (12.5 [13, 13, 14.5] cm)
> Finished circumference (at hem) 6 (6½, 7, 8)" (15 [16.5, 18, 20.5] cm)
> Finished length 10 (10, 10, 10½)" (25.5 [25.5, 25.5, 26.5] cm)

Model is shown in size S-M.

MATERIALS

> Classic Elite One Fifty (100% fine merino, each approximately 1¾ oz [50g] and 150yd [135m]), (3) light, in the following amounts and colors:
> 105 (115, 130, 140)yd (95 [105, 120, 130] m) / 1 ball, in color 7203 (pewter) MC
> 45 (50, 55, 60, 65)yd (40 [45, 50, 55, 60] m) / 1 ball, in color 7281 (ember glow) CC
> One set of 5 dpns, size 6 (4mm), or size needed to obtain gauge
> Stitch marker

GAUGE
24 stitches and 32 rows = 4" (10cm) in stockinette stitch

ARM WARMERS (MAKE 2)
The right and left are identical.

ARM

With MC, long-tail cast on 36 (40, 44, 48,) stitches. Distribute stitches evenly onto 4 dpns—9 (10, 11, 12) stitches on each needle.

Join to work in the round, being careful not to twist cast-on edge. Place marker at the beginning of the round.

Purl 3 rounds.

*With CC, knit 3 rounds.

With MC, knit 1 round, then purl 3 rounds.

Repeat from * once.

Cut CC after second CC section.

With MC, knit 1 round.

Decrease Round Over the first 3 stitches of needles 1 and 3, k1, ssk; over the last 3 stitches of needles 2 and 4, k2tog, k1—8 (9, 10, 11) stitches on each needle.

Knit 18 (18, 18, 20) rounds even.

Repeat Decrease Round—7 (8, 9, 10) stitches on each needle.

Knit 5 rounds.

Purl 3 rounds. Cut MC.

With CC, knit 17 rounds.

Increase Round Over the first 2 stitches of needles 1 and 3, k1, work lifted increase in next stitch, over the last 2 stitches of needles 2 and 4, work lifted increase in next stitch, k1—8 (9, 10, 11) stitches on each needle. Cut CC. With MC, knit 1 round.

Purl 3 rounds.

Knit 1 round.

XS (S-M) Sizes Only Repeat Increase Round—9 (10) stitches on each needle.

All Sizes Knit 8 rounds—9 (10, 10, 11) stitches on each needle, ending at marker.

HAND

Increase Round Work to last 2 stitches of needle 2, work lifted increase in next stitch, k1; at needle 3, k1, work lifted increase in second stitch—9 (10, 10, 11) stitches on needles 1 & 4; 10 (11, 11, 12) stitches on needles 2 and 3.

Knit 2 rounds.

Next Round Knit 1 round. AT THE SAME TIME, put last 4 (5, 5, 6) stitches of needle 2 and first 4 (5, 5, 6) stitches of needle 3 on a holder for thumb, cast on 2 stitches onto end of needle 2—9 (10, 10, 11) stitches on needles 1 and 4; 7 stitches on needles 2 and 3.

Distribute 32 (34, 34, 36) stitches evenly over 4 needles, and knit 7 (7, 7, 8) rounds.

Purl 2 rounds.

With CC, knit 3 rounds. Cut CC.

With MC, knit 1 round, then purl one round, then bind off.

Arm Warmers

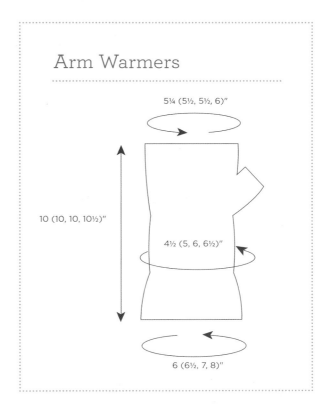

5¼ (5½, 5½, 6)"

10 (10, 10, 10½)"

4½ (5, 6, 6½)"

6 (6½, 7, 8)"

THUMB

Return to stitches on holder. Put 4 (5, 5, 6) stitches on needle 1 and 4 (5, 5, 6) stitches on needle 2. With MC and needle 3, pick up and knit 6 stitches along edge of hand—to produce inside edge of thumb—14 (16, 16, 18) stitches for thumb.

Knit 3 (3, 4, 4) rounds, then bind off.

✳ TECHNIQUE ✳

Combining colors with the textures of knitting can give a gorgeous result. But for a "clean" separation between the colors, a new color must *always* be introduced in stockinette (RS knit, WS purl). After that introduction, you can take work it as you wish!

Peaked Cap

DESIGNED BY CADDY

I knit this hat out of frustration at trying to find one that was both warm *and* looked good on me. I was so happy with this hat that I don't think I stopped wearing it until it started to smell . . . because I was sweating while trying to wear it in July! I then tried it on my mom (who swears no hat looks good on her), and of course it looked *amazing*. This was very exciting for us, because *never* has a hat looked good on *both* me and my mom. And I believe the guys will love it too! So here it is, shared with you, as it should be.

SKILL LEVEL
Easy

SIZES
> Woman's (Man's)
> Finished circumference (relaxed) 18 (19)" (45.5 [48.5]cm)
> Finished circumference (stretched) 20 (21)" (51 [53.5]cm)
> Finished height 7½ (8)" (19 [20.5]cm)

Model is shown in woman's size.

MATERIALS
> 42 (50)yd (38 [45]m) / 1 (1) skein Brown Sheep Company Burly Spun (100% wool, each approximately 4oz [114g] and 130yd [120m], in color 115 (oatmeal), (6) super bulky
> 2 size 15 (10mm) circular needles, 20" (51cm), or size needed to obtain gauge
> Stitch marker

GAUGE
10 stitches and 12 rows = 4" (10cm) in 1x1 rib

Hat

Long-tail cast on 44 (48) stitches.
Join to work in the round, being careful not to twist cast-on edge. Place marker to denote beginning of round.

Work 1x1 rib (* k1, p1; repeat from * to end) in rounds until piece measures 4½ (5)" (11.5 [12.5]cm).
First Decrease Round *Work 9 (10) stitches, k2tog (ssk), work 9 (10) stitches, ssk; repeat from * once.
Second Decrease Round *Work 8 (9) stitches, k2tog; repeat from * 3 times more.
Repeat second decrease round, working 1 less stitch between decreases each time, until 8 stitches remain.
Introduce second circular needle when needed.

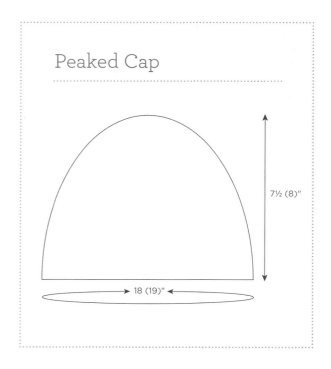

Peaked Cap

7½ (8)"

18 (19)"

✳ TECHNIQUE ✳

I suggest a second circular, rather than dpns, because dpns in this size are hard to come by. (If you can find them, and are more comfortable with them, by all means use them.) To work with two circulars, distribute stitches evenly over each needle. Call one "needle A" and the second "needle B." Use needle A to work the stitches of needle A, and use needle B to work the stitches of needle B.

Cut yarn.
Thread tapestry needle through last 8 stitches, remove needles, and pull tight.

FINISHING

PEAK

With WS facing, pick up and knit 23 (25) stitches across rim of Hat.

✳ TECHNIQUE ✳

The peak is worked on the WS to create a ridge on the RS.

Beginning and ending with p1, work 1x1 rib for 1 (RS) row.
Decrease Row (WS) Ssk, work rib last 2 stitches, k2tog.
Repeat Decrease Row twice more, then bind off in rib.

Hooded Scarf

DESIGNED BY CADDY

An alternative to the hat and scarf combo, this scarf actually looks like there is a really cool hooded sweater hiding under your coat. And it's warmer than a scarf and hat because there is no gap at the back of your neck. Super-warm and super-fashionable? Oh yes!

SKILL LEVEL
Easy

SIZES
> One size
> Height 9½" (24cm)
> Width (around) 19" (48.5cm)
> Length of scarves (before braiding) 24" (61cm)

MATERIALS
> 360yd (325m) / 4 skeins Misti International Misti Alpaca Chunky (100% baby alpaca, each approximately 3½ oz [100g] and 110yd [100m]), in color C815 (chartreuse mélange), (5) bulky
> One size 10½ (6.5mm) circular needle, or size needed to obtain gauge, 24" (61cm) or longer
> Cable needle
> 32" (81cm) elastic, ⅛" (3mm) wide

GAUGE
> 14 stitches and 20 rows = 4" (10cm) in simple cable
> 12 stitches and 16 rows = 4" (10cm) in seed stitch

STITCH PATTERNS
Simple Cable (over a multiple of 12 + 10 stitches)
(See chart)
Seed Stitch (over an odd number of stitches)
All Rows *K1, p1, repeat from * to last stitch, k1.

PATTERN NOTE
The Hood is knit first, then seamed along the center back. The scarf is knit by picking up along the Hood's neck edge, by casting on extra stitches at each edge, and then working down from these stitches.

HOOD

Long-tail cast on 70 stitches.

Beginning with row 1, work from simple cable chart until piece measures 9½" (24cm). End after working a WS row.

Bind off knitwise.

Fold Hood in half along cast-on edge. Sew folded cast-on edges together to form center back seam.

SCARVES

✳ TECHNIQUE ✳

Rather than one long scarf, there are 3 scarves (at each end) that are braided.

With RS facing and beginning at bound-off edge, pick up and knit 2 stitches for every 3 rows along entire neck edge of Hood.

Count stitches. Decrease evenly over center of next row, if needed, to an odd number of stitches.

*Next 2 Rows E-wrap cast on 72 stitches. Turn. Work seed stitch to end.

Continue in seed stitch to 1¾" (4.5cm). End after working a RS row.

Bind off 72 stitches in pattern at beginning of next 2 rows.

Repeat from * twice more, binding off all stitches at end of third scarf.

FINISHING

Loosely braid 3 scarf pieces of each side. Secure bottom of braids by wrapping and tying a piece of yarn around its end.

With WS facing, weave elastic along entire neck edge of Hood. Try the garment on, and pull elastic to achieve desired fit. Weave ends of elastic back along neck edge to center, and knot them together.

Hooded Scarf

9½"

20"

ATTACHED TO HOOD AT NECK EDGE

1¾"

5¼"

24"

24"

SIMPLE CABLE

8-ROW REPEAT

12-STITCH REPEAT

☐ knit on RS, purl on WS

● purl on RS, knit on WS

Slip next 2 stitches from left needle onto cn and hold at back, p2 from left needle, then k2 from cn

Slip next 2 stitches from left needle onto cn and hold at front, k2 from left needle, then p2 from cn

Add-On Afghan

DESIGNED BY SALLY

I wanted an afghan that could be started now, used in progress, and finished whenever. Hence this pattern which is more or less random, done in strips without an edging, started with the middle strip and worked to as many strips as desired, and possibly added onto later.

I think the color pattern of this afghan is fun, and I know that as a child I would have studied it to find its sequence—as I did a cherished afghan made by my grandmother.

SKILL LEVEL
Easy

SIZE
All measurements are approximate, after assembling, and before washing.
> Width 51" (129.5cm)
> Length 45" (114cm)

MATERIALS
Yarn amounts are approximate because the piece is worked randomly.
> Diamond Galway Highland Heather (100% wool, each approximately 3½ oz [100g] and 220yd [200m]), (4) medium, in following amounts and colors:
> 500yd (450m) / 3 balls each, in colors 700 (ruddy heather) C2, 638 (midnight blue) C3, 701 (teal) C4
> 300yd (270m) / 2 balls each, in colors 620 (claret) C1, 687 (forest) C5
> 100yd (90m) / 1 ball, in color 705 (moss) C6
> One size G-6 (4mm) crochet hook
> One pair size 9 (5.5mm) needles

GAUGE
Approximately 14 stitches and 24 rows (12 garter ridges) = 3" (7.5cm) in stitch pattern, before washing. *Gauge does not matter.*

STITCH PATTERN
All Rows Wyif slip 1 purlwise, knit to end.

PATTERN NOTE
The strips are knit to random numbers of rows in one color and then to random numbers of rows in another color: the pattern only gives guidelines for the lengths to which to knit. (To give specific lengths for color areas in each strip would have made the pattern too long.) You may also look at the photo for further guidance.

Afghan

STRIP 1
The afghan starts with the center strip.
With C1, crochet cast on 14 stitches.

✳ FLATTER & FIT ✳

The size given is for the sample (as written). You may, of course, knit it to any height and with any number of strips. Measurements and yarn amounts will vary accordingly.

This piece may stretch 1" (2.5cm) in width and as much as 5" (12.5cm) in length after washing.

✳ TECHNIQUE ✳

I used the crochet cast-on (see Glossary, page 167) because it mimics the bound-off and slip-stitch edges. You may substitute with any other cast-on. But if you use the long-tail, work an odd number of rows in the first color (because the long-tail cast-on already has one row of knitting worked).

*Work between 16 and 32 rows in C1.

You should always work an even number of rows in a color or you will get messy color changes.

Work 4, 6, or 8 rows in C2.

✳ TECHNIQUE ✳

Carry C1 up the side; work in C2 and C3 tails as you go (over the following row)—by knitting in the tail of the same color and weaving the tail of the alternate color. (We knit in tails of the same color because this won't show, but we have to weave in tails of alternate colors or they will show on the right side of the piece. See Glossary, page 167.)

Work between 16 and 32 rows in C1.
Work 4, 6, or 8 rows in C3.
Work between 16 and 32 rows in C1.
Work 4, 6, or 8 rows in C2.
Work 4, 6, or 8 rows in C3.
Repeat from * to 180 ridges (360 rows).
The strip will measure approximately 50" (127cm): it will shorten to approximately 45" (114cm) with assembly but will lengthen again after washing.
(Shorten or lengthen for finished length here.)
If you shortened or lengthened, count the number of ridges worked, and knit all following strips to the same number of ridges.

STRIPS 2 AND 3

These strips will attach on either side of the first strip. All subsequent pairs of strips will attach to the outsides of the previous strip. This will make the afghan symmetrical.
Work as Strip 1 but use C2 instead of C1, C3 instead of C2, and C4 instead of C3.
Begin these Strips with a different number of rows than you began Strip 1.

STRIPS 4 AND 5

Work as Strip 1 but as use C3 instead of C1, C4 instead of C2, C5 instead of C3.
Begin these Strips with a different number of rows than you began the adjoining Strips.

STRIPS 6 AND 7

Work as Strip 1 but use C4 instead of C1, C5 instead of C2, C6 instead of C3.
Begin these Strips with a different number of rows than you began the adjoining Strips.

STRIPS 8 AND 9

Work as Strip 1 but use C5 instead of C1, C6 instead of C2, C4 instead of C3.
Begin these Strips with a different number of rows than you began the adjoining Strips.

STRIPS 10 AND 11

Work as Strips 6 and 7.

STRIPS 12 AND 13

Work as Strips 4 and 5.

STRIPS 14 AND 15

Work as Strips 2 and 3.

STRIPS 16 AND 17

Work as Strip 1.

FINISHING

Join the Strips with colors as follows: begin with seams at either side of center in C1; as you work away from center, work seams in C2, then C3, then C4, then C5, then C4, then C3, then C2.

✳ TECHNIQUE ✳

The directions given are to join it with single crochet (because I like how it looks and because I don't have to add the extra step of slipping all the slip stitches onto needles). But if you prefer, you may join it with the 3-needle bind off (see Glossary, page 167).

To join Strips, work loosely and in single crochet as follows.

- Hold 2 strips with WS together, matching side edges to be joined
- Beginning at cast-on edge, insert crochet hook through inside edges of corresponding slip stitches (one from each Strip)
- Draw yarn through slip stitches—1 loop on hook

- Draw yarn through loop on hook—1 loop on hook
- * Insert hook through inside edges of next 2 slip stitches; draw yarn through—2 loops on hook
- Draw yarn through both loops—1 loop on hook
- Repeat from * to end
- Cut yarn, and draw through last loop.

Once the afghan is complete, strengthen final side edges by working single crochet through both slip stitches in main color of these strips and with WS facing.

Wash, as directed, in a wool-wash solution. Hang to dry over shower rod.

Architectural Shawl

DESIGNED BY SALLY

I absolutely love everything about this shawl—its style, its shape, its construction, the way this yarn hangs on the body—and the knitting was just sheer joy!

While this was intended for all us fashionable young things, I made one for my mother, who wore it every day, in bed or out. So it's not only a shawl but serves well for an extra layer of warmth when curled up on the couch or knitting in bed (and its shorter back suits this purpose).

SKILL LEVEL
Intermediate

SIZE
> S-M (L-2X)
> Width of triangle (at widest point) 56 (61)″ (142 [155]cm)
> Length of triangle (at tallest point) 23″ (58.5cm)
> Approximate center front length 22″ (56cm)
> Approximate center back length (with shawl collar turned over) 20″ (51cm)

Model is shown in size S-M.

MATERIALS
> 870 (950)yd (785 [855]m) / 4 skeins Shelridge Farm Soft Touch W4 (100% wool, each approximately 3½ oz [100g] and 220yd [200m]), in color Autumn Orange, medium
> One pair size 7 (4.5mm) needles, or size needed to obtain gauge
> One size G-6 (4mm) crochet hook
> 5 buttons, ¾″ (2cm) wide

GAUGE
> 10 stitches = 2″ (5cm) in garter stitch, before blocking
> 20 stitches and 36 rows (18 ridges) = 4″ (10cm) in garter stitch, taken over the second strip and before attaching the third, before blocking
> 19 stitches and 38 rows (19 ridges) = 4″ (10cm) in garter stitch, after completion and blocking

STITCH PATTERNS
Slip-Stitch Garter
RS Rows Knit.
WS Rows Wyif sl 1 p-wise, knit to last stitch, wyif sl 1 p-wise.

Joining Stitch Pattern
RS Rows K13 (14), skp (joining the last stitch of this strip to the previous strip). Turn.
WS Rows Wyif sl 1 p-wise, knit to last stitch, wyif sl 1 p-wise.
Final Row Bind off to 1 stitch on right needle and 2 stitches remaining on left needle; sl 1, k1, pass 2 stitches over, cut yarn, and draw through loop.

PATTERN NOTES
1. This shawl is done in strips of garter stitch—each just slightly less than (more than) 3″ (7.5cm) wide.
2. The first and all odd-numbered strips have ridges running horizontally; the second and all even-numbered strips have ridges running vertically.
3. The lower back edge is flat across the center 5 strips, and the back is shorter than the front. All other strips are made to be stair-stepped.
4. The shawl begins at center back. The right half is knit first, and the vertical pieces are knit bottom to top. The left half is knit last, and the vertical pieces are knit top to bottom. (This will make more sense when you do the work, and the schematic will help because it indicates in which direction each piece was knit.)

5. When one number appears, it applies to both sizes.
6. Go to www.sallymelvilleknits.com and click on "Books" to see a view of the back.

Shawl

STRIP 1, CENTER BACK STRIP
Crochet cast on 14 (15) stitches.

✳ TECHNIQUE ✳

The crochet cast-on (see Glossary, page 167) mimics the bound-off and slip-stitch edges. But you may substitute with the knitted cast-on instead.

Work slip-stitch garter to 109 ridges.

✳ TECHNIQUE ✳

The slip-stitch edge (see Glossary, page 167) is vitally important to the success of the project. Be very careful to slip the first and last stitches of every WS row. Perhaps mark the wrong side of the first strip to remind yourself. (After the second strip is begun, the RS and WS are quite obvious.)

End after working a WS row.

The piece may measure 25" (63.5cm) or slightly more. It will shorten to 23" (58.5cm) when the next piece is added.
(Shorten or lengthen for finished length here.)
If you alter length, your row counts at the ends of the following vertical pieces and your stitch counts for the following horizontal pieces will be different.
Bind off and cut yarn.

STRIP 2 (FIRST STRIP TO RIGHT OF CENTER BACK STRIP)
With WS facing and starting at beginning of bound-off edge of Strip 1, slip needle along entire edge, through bumps that sit closest to slip-stitch edge—110 bumps/stitches on needle.
Through all following directions, always slip needle through those bumps that sit closest to the slip-stitch edge.
With RS facing, begin slip-stitch garter.
Work to 13 (14) ridges. End after working a WS row.

STRIP 3
Insert crochet hook into first stitch on left needle; crochet cast on 14 (15) stitches—124 (125) stitches on left needle.

Architectural Shawl

ARROW INDICATES DIRECTION OF KNITTING.

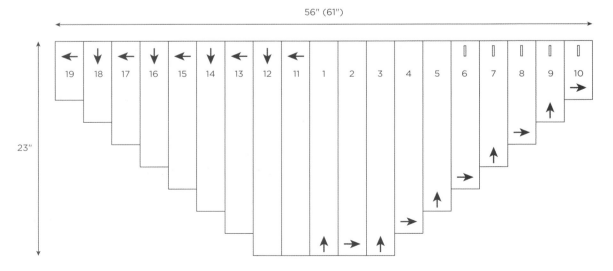

Work joining stitch pattern until 1 stitch remains from previous strip.

Finish with final row of joining stitch pattern.

STRIP 4

With WS facing and starting at beginning of bound-off edge of previous strip, slip needle through only 100 bumps—100 stitches on the needle.

You are not picking up the final 10 bumps—which would take you all the way to the cast-on edge. Stopping short will create the staggered edge.

With RS facing, begin slip-stitch garter.

Work to 13 (14) ridges. End after working a WS row.

Bind off 10 stitches, then slip stitch from right needle onto left—90 stitches on left needle.

This bind-off of 10 stitches will continue the staggered edge.

STRIP 5

Insert crochet hook into first stitch on left needle; crochet cast on 14 (15) stitches—104 (105) stitches on left needle.

Work joining stitch pattern until 1 stitch remains from previous strip.

Finish with final row of joining stitch pattern.

STRIP 6

Pick up bumps as Strip 4 to only 80 bumps—80 stitches on needle.

With RS facing, begin slip-stitch garter.

Work to 6 (7) ridges. End after working a WS row.

Buttonhole Row Knit to last 5 stitches; *wyif sl 1, wyib sl 1, psso—1 stitch bound off; sl 1, psso—2 stitches bound off; put single stitch back onto left needle; turn; wyib and cable cast-on method, cast on 1 stitch, cable cast on 1 more stitch but before putting stitch onto left needle bring yarn between needles and to front; turn; * k3.

Work to 13 (14) ridges. End after working a WS row.

Bind off 10 stitches, then slip stitch from right needle onto left—70 stitches on left needle.

STRIP 7

Insert crochet hook into first stitch on left needle; crochet cast on 14 (15) stitches—84 (85) stitches on left needle.

**Work joining stitch pattern until only 4 stitches remain on left needle. End after working a WS row.

Buttonhole Row K6 (7), make buttonhole as * to * of Strip 6, k5, skp.

Continue with joining stitch pattern until 1 stitch

remains from previous strip.

Finish with final row of joining stitch pattern.

STRIP 8

Pick up bumps as Strip 4 to only 60 bumps—60 stitches on needle.

With RS facing, begin slip-stitch garter.

Work to 6 (7) ridges. End after working a RS row.

Buttonhole Row Knit to last 5 stitches, make buttonhole as * to * of Strip 6, k3.

Work to 13 (14) ridges. End after working a WS row.

Bind off 10 stitches, then slip stitch from right needle onto left—50 stitches on left needle.

STRIP 9

Insert crochet hook into first stitch on left needle; crochet cast on 14 (15) stitches—64 (65) stitches on left needle.

Work as Strip 7 from ** to end.

STRIP 10

Pick up bumps as Strip 4 to only 40 bumps—40 stitches on needle.

With RS facing, begin slip-stitch garter.

Work 6 (7) ridges. End after working a RS row.

Buttonhole Row Knit to last 5 stitches, make buttonhole as * to * of Strip 6, knit to end.

Continue to 12 (13) ridges. End after working a WS row.

Bind off all 40 stitches.

STRIP 11 (FIRST STRIP TO LEFT OF CENTER BACK STRIP)

With WS facing and starting at cast-on edge of Strip 1, slip needle along entire edge, through bumps that sit closest to the slip-stitch edge—110 bumps/stitches on needle.

With RS facing, begin slip-stitch garter.

The beginning of all RS rows is at the top of the piece.

Work to 13 (14) ridges.

End after working a WS row.

STRIP 12

Insert crochet hook into first stitch on left needle; crochet-cast on 14 (15) stitches—124 (125) stitches on left needle.

Beginning with a RS row, work joining stitch pattern until 1 stitch remains from previous strip.

You are working top to bottom.

Finish with final row of joining stitch pattern.

STRIP 13

With WS facing and beginning 10 ridges up from bound-off edge of previous strip, slip needle through 100 bumps—100 stitches on needle.

***With RS facing, begin slip-stitch garter.

Work to 13 (14) ridges. End after working a WS row.

STRIP 14

Insert crochet hook into first stitch on left needle; crochet cast on 14 (15) stitches—104 (105) stitches on left needle.

****Beginning with RS row, work joining stitch pattern until 11 stitches remain from previous strip. End after working a WS row—25 (26) stitches on left needle.

Final Row Bind off 12 (13), sl 1, k1, pass 2 stitches over, bind off to end.

Binding off—instead of joining—the final 10 stitches from the previous strip continues the staggered edge.

STRIP 15

Pick up bumps as Strip 13 to only 80 bumps—80 stitches on needle.

Work as Strip 13 from *** to end.

STRIP 16

Insert crochet hook into first stitch on left needle; crochet cast on 14 (15) stitches—84 (85) stitches on left needle.

Work as Strip 14 from **** to end.

STRIP 17

Pick up bumps as Strip 13 to only 60 bumps—60 stitches on needle.

Work as Strip 13 from *** to end.

STRIP 18

Insert crochet hook into first stitch on left needle; crochet cast on 14 (15) stitches—64 (65) stitches on left needle.

Work as Strip 14 from **** to end.

STRIP 19

Pick up bumps as Strip 13 to only 40 bumps–40 stitches on needle.

Work as Strip 13 from *** to end.

Bind off all 40 stitches.

FINISHING

Sew buttons to match placement of buttonholes.

Block piece well (by washing as directed in a wool-wash solution.) Dry flat.

Try the shawl on, with collar turned over as desired.

If needed, stitch the sides of the collar down at the shoulders.

Cardilero

DESIGNED BY CADDY

My friend Pauline actually helped me name this piece. Because it's a cross between a bolero and a cardigan, I was going to call it a Bordigan. . . . Bordigan? What was I thinking?! Thank you, Pauline.

SKILL LEVEL
Intermediate

SIZES
> XS (S, M, L 1X)
All measurements are after blocking.
> Finished bust 36 (40, 44, 48, 52)" (91 [101.5, 112, 122, 132]cm)
> Finished shoulder width 13 (14, 15½, 16½, 18)" (33 [35.5, 39.5, 42, 45.5]cm)
Model is shown in size XS.

✳ FLATTER & FIT ✳

The finished bust measurement is approximate, because the right front can overlap the left front as little or as much as desired.

The back of the garment will stretch, when worn, to the shoulder width and sleeve length indicated.

To make the back lie flat when worn, pull the fronts forward at the underarms before pinning.

MATERIALS

> 430 (470, 540, 590, 640)yd (390 [425, 490, 530, 580]m) / 3 (3, 4, 4, 4) skeins Tahki Yarns Donegal Tweed (100% pure new wool, each approximately 3½ oz [100g] and 183yd [167m]), in color 810 (fuchsia), (4) medium
> One size 8 (5mm) circular needle, or size needed to obtain gauge, 20" (51cm) or longer
> Cable needle
> Kilt or shawl pin

GAUGE

> 18 stitches and 24 rows = 4" (10cm) in 1x1 rib
> 16 stitches and 22 rows = 4" (10cm) in stockinette stitch
> 16 stitches and 20 rows = 4" (10cm) in cardilero cable

Cardilero

LEFT FRONT

Cast on 61 (65, 69, 75, 81) stitches.
Work 1x1 rib (beginning and ending all RS rows with p1 and all WS rows with k1) for 9 rows.
*Next Row (RS) [P1, k1] twice; p15 (17, 19, 22, 24); work row 1 of cable chart over 26 stitches; p12 (14, 16, 19, 23); [k1, p1] twice.
Next Row (WS) [K1, p1] twice; k12 (14, 16, 19, 23); work row 2 of cable chart over 26 stitches; k15 (17, 19, 22, 24); [p1, k1] twice.*
Continue as established until Left Front measures 9 (10, 11, 12, 13)" (23 [25.5, 28, 30.5, 33]cm). End after working a WS row.

LEFT ARMHOLE

Continue rib, RSS, and cable as established, through shaping.
Next Row (RS) Work 10 (12, 14, 14, 16) stitches; bind off 36 (38, 40, 42, 44) stitches; work to end.
Next Row (WS) Work 15 (15, 15, 19, 21) stitches, e-wrap cast on 36 (38, 40, 42, 44) stitches, work to end.

BACK

Continuing rib, RSS, and cable as established (see Left Front, * to *), work until Back measures 9 (10, 11, 12, 13)" (23 [25.5, 28, 30.5, 33]cm). End after working a WS row.

Cardilero

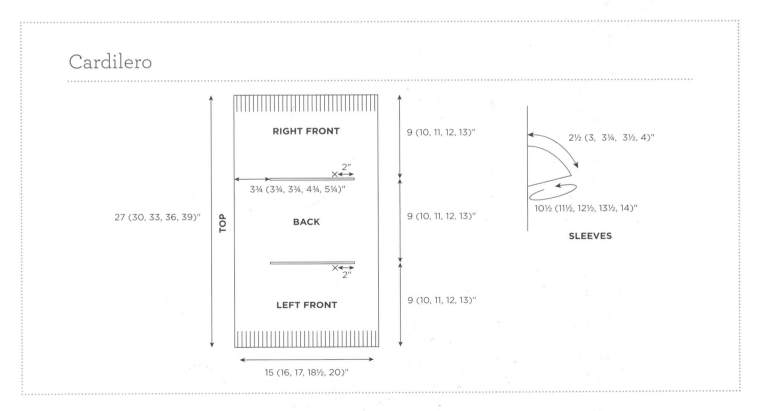

RIGHT FRONT

2"

3¾ (3¾, 3¾, 4¾, 5¼)"

BACK

LEFT FRONT

2"

27 (30, 33, 36, 39)"

TOP

9 (10, 11, 12, 13)"

9 (10, 11, 12, 13)"

9 (10, 11, 12, 13)"

15 (16, 17, 18½, 20)"

2½ (3, 3¼, 3½, 4)"

10½ (11½, 12½, 13½, 14)"

SLEEVES

RIGHT ARMHOLE

Work as Left Armhole.

RIGHT FRONT

Continuing rib, RSS, and cable as established (see Left Front, * to *), work until Right Front measures 7½ (8½, 9½, 10½, 11½)" (19 [21.5, 24, 26.5, 29]cm).
Work 1x1 rib for 9 rows, then bind off in rib.

SLEEVES

With RS facing and beginning at underarm as marked by "X"s on schematic, pick up and knit around armhole opening as follows: 4 stitches for every 5 bound-off stitches or cast-on stitches, and 2 stitches—approximately 62 (65, 68, 72, 75) stitches.

✴ TECHNIQUE ✴

When picking up and knitting (see Glossary, page 167), you will not get holes if you always insert your needle into spaces so that you then see two threads on your needle.

Count stitches. Over the next row increase or decrease evenly (as needed) to a multiple of 5 stitches.
Work back and forth in 1x1 rib for 1 (2, 3, 4, 5) row(s).
Next Row Continuing in 1x1 rib, bind off 5 stitches at beginning of next row.

✴ TECHNIQUE ✴

For a neat finished edge, always bind off in pattern.

Repeat last row until 0 stitches remain.

FINISHING

SLEEVE EDGING

With RS facing, pick up and knit 4 (4, 4, 4, 5) stitches for every 5 (5, 5, 5, 6) bound-off stitches along Sleeve edge—approximately 48 (52, 56, 60, 63) stitches.
Knit 1 row, then purl 1 row, then bind off loosely and knitwise.

Sew Sleeve seams.
Block well (by washing as directed in a wool-wash solution). Dry flat.

Cardilero

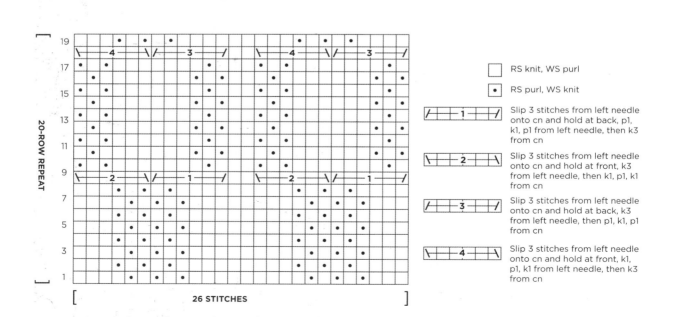

Chart legend:

- □ RS knit, WS purl
- ▪ RS purl, WS knit
- 1 — Slip 3 stitches from left needle onto cn and hold at back, p1, k1, p1 from left needle, then k3 from cn
- 2 — Slip 3 stitches from left needle onto cn and hold at front, k3 from left needle, then k1, p1, k1 from cn
- 3 — Slip 3 stitches from left needle onto cn and hold at back, k3 from left needle, then p1, k1, p1 from cn
- 4 — Slip 3 stitches from left needle onto cn and hold at front, k1, p1, k1 from left needle, then k3 from cn

20-ROW REPEAT

26 STITCHES

Center-Paneled Vest / Sweater

DESIGNED BY SALLY

This piece was based on a garment I bought, loved, and could not stop wearing. It has many features I know to be flattering: a shorter front that makes us look taller; a longer back that covers any sins lurking there; a not-straight hem that diminishes width; a slight A-line that frames the body nicely; and wide shoulders that draw the eye up and out. All good stuff!

The red version looks like it has sleeves, because the top underneath is close to the same color. But it does not have sleeves . . . and the sleeves really are optional. I love it as a vest and equally as a sweater! I already own one of each and am contemplating more.

SKILL LEVEL
Intermediate

SIZE
> Length at side seams 23¾ (24¼, 24¾, 25¼, 25¾)" (60.5 [61.5, 62.5, 64, 65.5]cm)
> Length at center back 26½ (27, 27½, 28, 28½)" (67.5 [68.5, 70, 71, 72]cm)
> Length at center front (not including collar) 19½ (20, 20½, 21, 21½)" (49.5 [51, 52, 53.5, 54.5]cm)
> Finished hem 38½ (42½, 46½, 50½, 54½)" (98 [108, 118, 128.5, 138]cm)
> Finished bust 36½ (40½, 44½, 48½, 52)" (91.5 [103, 113, 123, 132]cm)
> Shoulder width 17 (18, 19, 20, 21½)" (43 [45.5, 48, 51, 54.5]cm)
> Sleeve length (for sleeved version only) 29½ (30, 30, 31, 31½)" (75 [76, 77.5, 79, 80]cm)

Model is shown in size M.

MATERIALS
For vest—sides and back
> 540 (600, 660, 720, 780)yd ([485, 540, 595, 650, 700]m) / 7 (8, 9, 9, 10) skeins Mirasol Miski (100% baby llama, each approximately 1¾ oz [50g] and 82yd [75m]), in color 108 (copper), (4) medium

For vest—center front panel
> 165 (170, 175, 180, 185)yd (150 [153, 160, 162, 165]m) / 1 skein Diamond Luxury Collection Alpaca Prima

(100% alpaca, each approximately 1¾ oz [50g] and 185yd [169m]), in color 2095 (red brick), **①** super-fine

For sweater—sides, back, and sleeves

> 885 (985, 1085, 1180, 1280)yd (800 [885, 975, 1060, 1150]m) / 5 (5, 6, 6, 7) skeins Punta Yarns Merisoft Space Dyed (100% merino, each approximately 3½ oz [100g] and 197yd [178m]), in color NM 1800 (chartreuse), **④** medium

For sweater—center front panel

> 165 (170, 175, 180, 185)yd (150 [153, 160, 162, 165]m) / 1 skein Punta Yarns MeriSock Handpainted (95% merino wool, 5% nylon, each approximately 3½ oz [100g] and 463yd [417m]), in color HP72 (chartreuse and navy), **①** superfine
> One pair size 9 (5.5m) needles or size needed to obtain gauge in heavier yarn
> One pair size 1½–2 (2.5–2.75mm) needles, or size needed to obtain gauge in finer yarn
> One spare circular needle (to use as holder)

GAUGE

> 15 stitches and 22 rows = 4" (10cm) in heavier yarn and stockinette stitch, over larger needles and after blocking
> Approximately 33 stitches and 44 rows = 4" (10cm) in finer yarn and stockinette stitch, over smaller needles and after blocking

PATTERN NOTES

1. The front panel is done in a finer yarn and in a darker, coordinating color.
2. Don't worry if you don't get row gauge in the finer yarn. If you get close, the seaming will pull it to the right length. If you aren't close, see Finishing for alternative directions.
3. The vest's armholes roll under and will make the vest's shoulders a little narrower than the gauge or schematic would suggest.
4. The collar rolls to the right side and exposes its seam allowances; this is an intended part of the design.

Vest

BACK

SHORT-ROW SHAPED HEM

With larger needles and heavier yarn, long-tail cast on 78 (84, 92, 100, 106) stitches.

Next (WS) Short Row P48 (54, 62, 70, 76). Turn—30 stitches left behind.

Next (RS) Short Row Slip 1 purlwise, k22 (28, 36, 44, 50). Turn.

Always sl 1 p-wise, and do not move the yarn from where it would be to work the row—at the back for a knit row, at the front for a purl row.

Next (WS) Short Row Sl 1, p27 (33, 41, 49, 55). Turn.

Next (RS) Short Row Sl 1, k32 (38, 46, 54, 60). Turn.

Next (WS) Short Row Sl 1, p37 (43, 51, 59, 65). Turn.

Next 6 Short Rows Sl 1, work to 5 stitches past previous short row (adding 5 stitches each time and continuing in stockinette stitch). Turn.

Next (RS) Short Row Sl 1, k72 (78, 86, 94, 100).

Next Row P78 (84, 92, 100, 106).

Continue in stockinette stitch until sides measure 3" (7.5cm). End after working a WS row.

SHAPE SIDES

*Decrease Row K1, skp, knit to last 3 stitches, k2tog, k1.

Continue until sides measure 3″ (7.5cm) past previous decrease. End after working a WS row.

(Shorten or lengthen by working fewer or more rows between decreases.)

Repeat from * 3 times more—70 (76, 84, 92, 98) stitches.

Work even until sides measure 15″ (38cm). End after working a WS row.

(Shorten or lengthen for finished length here.)

SHAPE ARMHOLE

Bind off 2 (2, 3, 4, 5) stitches at beginning of next 2 rows—66 (72, 78, 84, 88) stitches.

Decrease Row K1, skp, knit to last 3 stitches, k2tog, k1.

Work 1 WS row.

Repeat last 2 rows 0 (1, 2, 3, 3) time(s) more—64 (68, 72, 76, 80) stitches.

Work even until armhole measures 7½ (8, 8½, 9, 9½)″ (19 [20.5, 21.5, 23, 24]cm). End after working a WS row.

SHAPE SHOULDER

Bind off 1 (2, 3, 3, 3) stitch(es) at beginning of next 4 rows, then 2 (2, 2, 3, 4) stitches at beginning of next 4 rows—52 stitches.

Put remaining stitches onto spare circular needle (for collar.)

LEFT FRONT

SHORT-ROW SHAPED HEM

With larger needles and heavier yarn, long-tail cast on 29 (33, 37, 40, 44) stitches.

Next Row Purl.

Next RS Short Row K6 (10, 14, 17, 21). Turn.

Next Row Sl 1, p5 (9, 13, 16, 20).

Next RS Short Row K8 (12, 16, 19, 23). Turn.

Next Row Sl 1, p7 (11, 15, 18, 22). Turn.

Next 4 RS Short Rows Knit to 2 stitches past previous short row (adding 2 stitches each time).

Next 3 WS Rows Sl 1, purl to end.

Next WS Row Sl 1, p15 (19, 23, 26, 30).

Next RS Short Row K17 (21, 25, 28, 32). Turn.

Next WS Row Sl 1, p16 (20, 24, 27, 31).

Next 4 RS Short Rows Knit to 1 stitch past previous short row (adding 1 stitch each time).

Next 3 WS Rows Sl 1, purl to end.

Next WS Row Sl 1, p20 (24, 28, 31, 35).

Next RS Row K29 (33, 37, 40, 44).

Continue working all stitches in stockinette stitch until side measures same length as Back to armhole. End after working a WS row.

SHAPE ARMHOLE

Bind off 2 (2, 3, 4, 5) stitches at beginning of next row—27 (31, 34, 36, 39) stitches.

Work 1 WS row.

Decrease Row (RS) K1, skp, knit to end.

Repeat last 2 rows 1 (3, 4, 4, 5) time(s) more—25 (27, 29, 31, 33) stitches.

Work even until armhole measures same length as Back to shoulder. End after working a WS row.

SHAPE SHOULDER

Bind off 1 (2, 3, 3, 3) stitch(es) at beginning of next 2 armhole edges, then 2 (2, 2, 3, 4) stitches at beginning of next 2 armhole edges—19 stitches.

Put remaining stitches, RS facing, onto left end of spare needle (for collar).

RIGHT FRONT

SHORT-ROW SHAPED HEM

With larger needles and heavier yarn, long-tail cast on 29 (33, 37, 40, 44) stitches.

Next Short Row P6 (10, 14, 17, 21). Turn.

Next RS Row Sl 1, k5 (9, 13, 15, 20). Turn.

Next Short Row P8 (12, 16, 19, 23). Turn.

Next RS Row Sl 1, k7 (11, 15, 18, 22). Turn.

Next 4 WS Short Rows Purl to 2 stitches past previous short row (adding 2 stitches each time).

Next 3 RS Rows Sl 1, knit to end.

Next RS Row Sl 1, k15 (19, 23, 26, 30).

Next WS Short Row P17 (21, 25, 28, 32). Turn.

Next RS Row Sl 1, k16 (20, 24, 27, 31).

Next 4 WS Short Rows Purl to 1 stitch past previous short row (adding 1 stitch each time).

Next 3 RS Rows Sl 1, knit to end.

Next RS Row Sl 1, k20 (24, 28, 31, 35).

Next WS Row P29 (33, 37, 40, 44).

Continue working all stitches in stockinette stitch until side measures same length as Back to armhole. End after working a RS row.

SHAPE ARMHOLE

Bind off 2 (2, 3, 4, 5) stitches at beginning of next row—27 (31, 34, 36, 39) stitches.

Decrease Row (RS) Knit to last 3 stitches, k2tog, k1. Work 1 WS row.

Repeat last 2 rows 1 (3, 4, 4, 5) time(s) more—25 (27, 29, 31, 33) stitches.

Work even until armhole measures same length as Back to shoulder. End after working a RS row.

SHAPE SHOULDER

Bind off 1 (2, 3, 3, 3) stitch(es) at beginning of next 2 armhole edges, then 2 (2, 2, 3, 4) stitches at beginning of next 2 armhole edges—19 stitches. End after working a WS row.

Do not cut yarn.

COLLAR

Beginning with RS facing and Right Front, work as follows.

- Knit over stitches of Right Front to last stitch
- Sl 1 (last stitch of Right Front), k1 from Back, psso (joining last stitch of Right Front to first stitch of Back)
- Knit over stitches of Back to last stitch
- K2tog (joining last stitch of Back with first stitch of Left Front)
- Knit across remaining stitches of Left Front —88 stitches.

Continue in stockinette stitch over stitches of collar until collar measures 8" (20.5cm).

(Shorten or lengthen for finished collar height here.)

Bind off.

CENTER FRONT PANEL

With smaller needles and finer yarn, long-tail cast on 33 stitches.

Leave a long tail for seaming.

Count rows along edge of either Front, including collar. Beginning with a purl row, work in stockinette stitch until Center Front Panel is twice the number of rows as Front edge.

If your row gauge in the finer yarn does not give this two-to-one relationship, knit the Center Front Panel to the same length as both Front panels, and then seam in whatever proportion is demanded.

Bind off on a purl row.

Leave a long tail for seaming.

FINISHING

Sew side and shoulder seams.

With long tails, sew Center Front Panel to Right and Left Fronts, taking half a stitch from edge of Right and Left Fronts and 1 stitch from edge of Center Front Panel into seam allowance.

✳ TECHNIQUE ✳

Taking only half a stitch into the seam allowance of the heavier yarn will balance its seam allowance with the full stitch seam allowance of the finer yarn.

Block, pinning or steaming edges flat.

SLEEVES (OPTIONAL)

With larger needles and heavier yarn, long-tail cast on 28 (28, 32, 32, 36) stitches.

Beginning with a (WS) purl row, work in stockinette stitch for 5 rows.

***Increase Row (RS)** K1, work lifted increase in next stitch, knit to last 2 stitches, work lifted increase in next stitch, k1.

Work 7 (5, 5, 3, 3) rows even.

Repeat from * 10 (12, 12, 14, 14) times more—50 (54, 58, 62, 66) stitches.

Work even until piece measures 17½ (17, 16½, 16, 15½)" (44.5 [43, 42, 40.5, 39.5]cm). End after working a WS row.

SLEEVE CAP

Bind off 2 (2, 3, 4, 5) stitches at beginning of next 2 rows—46 (50, 52, 54, 56) stitches.

Decrease Row (RS) K1, skp, knit to last 3 stitches, k2tog, k1.

Work 1 WS row.

Repeat last 2 rows 7 (9, 10, 11, 12) times more—30 stitches.

Bind off 2 stitches at beginning of next 2 rows.

Bind off 4 stitches at beginning of next 2 rows.

Bind off remaining 18 stitches.

Sew Sleeves into armholes.

Sew Sleeve seams.

Center-Paneled Vest / Sweater

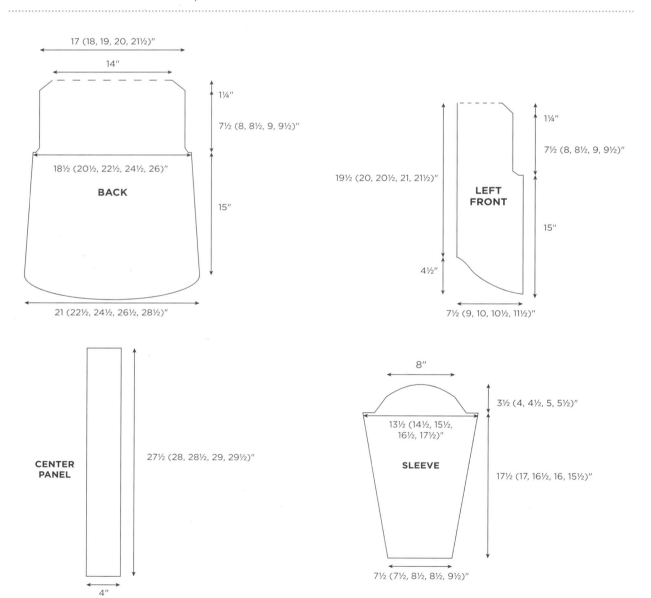

Christmas Morning Sweater

DESIGNED BY CADDY

You know that sweater you really want to pull on for Christmas morning (because it's so cozy) and not have to take off for Christmas dinner for the exact same reason? All too often that "cozy" morning sweater translates to "homely" after 3 p.m. The following sweater is my answer to the cozy sweater that not only stays cozy but gets mysteriously more and more gorgeous the more comfortable you become in it. Because the cowl neck is separate, you could wear it without in the morning but then throw it on for the evening. I bet the men in your family won't even notice you're wearing the same sweater.

SKILL LEVEL
Easy

SIZES
> XS (S, M, L, 1X)
> Finished circumference, at bust 33 (37, 41, 45, 49)" (84 [94, 104, 114.5, 124.5]cm)
> Finished circumference, at waist 29 (33, 37, 41, 45)" (73.5[84, 94, 104, 114]cm)
> Finished length 20 (20½, 21, 22, 22½)" (51 [52, 53.5, 56, 57]cm)
> Finished waist length 15 (15½, 16, 17, 17½)" (38 [39.5, 40.5, 43, 44.5]cm)
> Finished shoulder width 14 (15, 15, 16, 17)" (35.5 [38, 38, 40.5, 43]cm)

> Finished sleeve length 31 (32, 32½, 33½, 34)" (79 [81, 82.5, 85, 86]cm)

Model is shown in size S.

MATERIALS
> 1035 (1150, 1265, 1380, 1495)yd (935 [1035, 1140, 1245, 1345]m) / 9 (10, 11, 12, 13) balls Sublime Kid Mohair (60% kid mohair, 35% nylon, 5% extra fine merino, each approximately ⅞oz [25g] and 122yd [112m]), in color 0069 (mouse), (4) medium
> One size 8 (5mm) circular needle, or size needed to obtain gauge, 20" (51cm) or longer
> One pair size 6 (4mm) needles, or size needed to obtain gauge
> One pair size 3 (3.25mm) needles
> 2 stitch holders
> 2 stitch markers

GAUGE
> 18 stitches and 24 rows = 4" (10cm) in 1x1 rib, over largest needles
> 20 stitches and 28 rows = 4" (10cm) in stockinette stitch, over middle-sized needles
> 28 stitches and 34 rows = 4" (10cm) in 1x1 rib, over smallest needles
> 18 stitches and 24 rows = 4" (10cm) in stockinette stitch, over largest needles

✳ FLATTER & FIT ✳

Sleeve length is measured from center body to end of sleeve. For more information, see Glossary, page 167.

PATTERN NOTES

1. A circular needle is required (even though most of the garment is knit flat) for the neck edging and for the collar (which is knit in the round).
2. The collar is made to be worn with the narrower end down.
3. See page 10 for the sweater without the collar.

Sweater

BACK

With largest needle, cast on 76 (86, 96, 104, 114) stitches.

Work 1x1 rib for 6" (15cm). End after working a WS row.

(Shorten or lengthen for finished length here.)

Change to middle-sized needles, and work in stockinette stitch for 2" (5cm). End after working a WS row.

Change to largest needle, and work 1x1 rib for 5½" (14cm). End after working a WS row.

(Shorten or lengthen for waist length here.)

SHAPE ARMHOLE

Continue in rib as established through all following shaping.

Bind off 3 (4, 6, 8, 10) stitches at beginning of next 2 rows—70 (78, 84, 88, 94) stitches.

Decrease Row (RS) K1, ssk, work to last 3 stitches, k2tog, p1.

Work 1 row even.

Repeat last 2 rows 1 (3, 6, 7, 8) time(s) more—66 (70, 70, 72, 76) stitches.

(Widen or narrow for shoulder width by working fewer or more decreases.)

Continue even until armhole measures 6½ (7, 7½, 8½, 9)" (16.5 [18, 19, 21.5, 23]cm). End after working a WS row.

SHAPE RIGHT SHOULDER AND BACK NECK

Bind off 5 (5, 5, 6, 5) stitches, work to 15 (17, 17, 17, 20) stitches on right needle. Put next 26 stitches on holder (for Back neck). Turn.

*Bind off 1 stitch at neck edge, work to end.

Bind off 4 (5, 5, 5, 6) stitches at armhole edge, work to end.

Bind off 1 stitch at neck edge, work to end.

Bind off 5 (5, 5, 5, 6) stitches at armhole edge, work to end.

Work 1 row even.

Bind off remaining 4 (5, 5, 5, 6) stitches.

SHAPE LEFT SHOULDER AND BACK NECK

Work 1 RS row over remaining 20 (22, 22, 23, 25) stitches.

Bind off 5 (5, 5, 6, 5) stitches at armhole edge, work to end.

Work as Shape Right Shoulder and Back Neck from * to end.

FRONT

Work as Back through Shape Armhole to end of decreases—66 (70, 70, 72, 76) stitches.

(Widen or narrow for shoulder width as for Back.)

Continue even until armhole measures 5½ (6, 6½, 7½, 8)" (14 [15, 16.5, 19, 20.5]cm). End after working a WS row.

SHAPE LEFT FRONT NECK

Next Row (RS) Work to 25 (27, 27, 28, 30) stitches on right needle. Put next 16 stitches on holder (for Front neck). Turn.

*Shape neck by binding off as follows: 2 stitches twice, then 1 stitch 3 times—18 (20, 20, 21, 23) stitches. Work 2 rows even after final neck bind off.

SHAPE LEFT FRONT SHOULDER

Shape shoulder by binding off as follows: 5 (5, 5, 6, 5) stitches once, 4 (5, 5, 5, 6) stitches once, 5 (5, 5, 5, 6) stitches once, then final 4 (5, 5, 5, 6) stitches—0 stitches.

SHAPE RIGHT FRONT NECK AND SHOULDER

With RS facing, return to remaining 25 (27, 27, 28, 30) stitches.
Work 2 rows even.
Work as Shape Left Front Neck (through Shape Left Front Shoulder) from * to end.

SLEEVES

With smallest needles, cast on 38 (42, 46, 50, 54) stitches.
Work 1x1 rib for 7" (18cm). End after working a WS row.
Change to largest needles, and work in stockinette stitch for 2 rows.

✳ TECHNIQUE ✳

Work all increases as lifted increases (see Glossary, page 167). This is the best increase for stockinette stitch.

Increase Row (RS) *K1, increase 1 in next stitch; repeat from * 3 (3, 4, 5, 4) times more; knit to last 8 (8, 10, 12, 10) stitches; **increase 1 in next stitch, k1; repeat from ** to end—46 (50, 56, 62, 64) stitches.
Continue in stockinette stitch until Sleeve measures 13" (33cm).
(Shorten or lengthen for sleeve length here.)
Change to smallest needles, and work 1x1 rib until Sleeve measures 16" (40.5cm). End after working a WS row.
Change to largest needles, and work in stockinette stitch for 2 rows.

Increase Row (RS) *K1, increase 1 in next stitch; repeat from * 3 (4, 4, 7, 8) times more; knit to last 8 (10, 10, 16, 18) stitches; **increase 1 in next stitch, k1; repeat from ** to end—54 (60, 66, 78, 82) stitches.
Continue in stockinette stitch until Sleeve measures 20½" (52cm). End after working a WS row.

SHAPE SLEEVE CAP

Continue in stockinette stitch to end of Sleeve.
Bind off 3 (4, 6, 8, 10) stitches at beginning of next 2 rows—48 (52, 54, 62, 62).
Decrease Row (RS) K1, ssk, knit to last 3 stitches, k2tog, k1.
Purl 1 row.
Repeat the last 2 rows 10 (12, 13, 17, 17) times more—26 stitches.
Bind off 2 stitches at beginning of next 2 rows.
Bind off 4 stitches at beginning of next 2 rows.
Bind off remaining 14 stitches.

FINISHING

Sew shoulder seams.
Sew in Sleeves.
Sew Sleeve and side seams.

NECK EDGING

With largest needle and RS facing, begin at a shoulder seam to pick up and knit as follows:
- 1 stitch for every row (along straight edges)
- 1 stitch for every bound-off stitch
- 1 stitch for every 2-row step between bound-off stitches
- 1 stitch for every stitch on holder

—approximately 84 stitches.
Count stitches. Decrease evenly over next row (if needed) to achieve an even number of stitches.

INSPIRATION

I really wanted to experiment with the sleeves of this relatively simple sweater so they would be more interesting than a standard stockinette stitch sleeve. The result is a fairly long sleeve so that you can wear the looser, stockinette stitch sections bloused while the ribbed sections sit fitted on the arm.

Christmas Morning Sweater

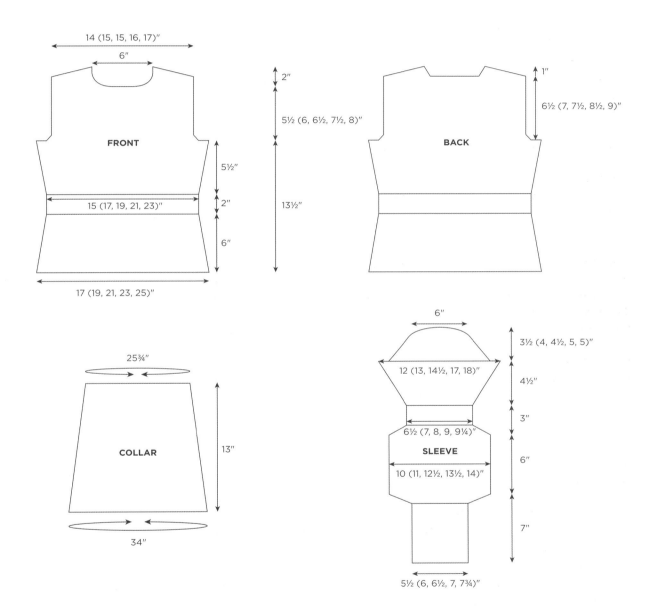

FRONT

14 (15, 15, 16, 17)"

6"

2"

5½ (6, 6½, 7½, 8)"

5½"

15 (17, 19, 21, 23)"

2"

6"

13½"

17 (19, 21, 23, 25)"

BACK

1"

6½ (7, 7½, 8½, 9)"

COLLAR

25¾"

13"

34"

SLEEVE

6"

3½ (4, 4½, 5, 5)"

12 (13, 14½, 17, 18)"

4½"

6½ (7, 8, 9, 9¼)"

3"

10 (11, 12½, 13½, 14)"

6"

7"

5½ (6, 6½, 7, 7¾)"

Join to work in the round, and place marker at beginning of round.
Work 1x1 rib for 2 rounds.
Bind off loosely and in rib.

COLLAR (SEPARATE)

With largest needle, cast on 152 stitches.
Join to work in the round, being careful not to twist cast-on edge. Place marker at beginning of round.
Beginning with k1, work 1x1 rib for 76 stitches, place second marker, work 1x1 rib to end of round.
Continue in 1x1 rib for 3 rounds, ending at first marker.
First Decrease Round Ssk, work to marker, ssk, work to end.

✴ TECHNIQUE ✴

When we decrease in rib, it throws our ribbing off—until the next decrease. It is my preference to have 2 knits (rather than 2 purls) when the ribbing is "off." So, in the first decrease, the knit stitch "overrides" the purl: hence the ssk. Then in the next decrease, we absorb the extra knit stitch: hence the p2tog.

Continue in rib for 3 rounds.
Second Decrease Round K1, p2tog, work to marker, k1, p2tog, work to end.
Continue in rib for 3 rounds.
Repeat last 8 rounds until piece measures approximately 13" (33cm). Bind off loosely in rib.

Sean's Fingerless Gloves

DESIGNED BY SALLY

I was sharing dinner with my Boston friend, Sean, and asked what I could do for the guys in a book devoted to winter and warmth. He said "Not a scarf. How about fingerless gloves?" So here they are!

SKILL LEVEL
Intermediate

SIZE
> One size, two yarns
> Circumference at cuff and hand 8 (8½)" (20.5 [21.5]cm)
> Circumference at wrist and fingers 7 (7½)" (18 [19]cm)
> Finished length 8" (20.5cm)

✳ TECHNIQUE ✳
A heavier yarn (like the Iro, shown on the next page) will produce a larger glove even over the same size needles than a lighter yarn (like the Maxi Tosca, shown to the right). This is fine, because the heavier yarn needs more ease—since it fills in more of the glove's circumference.

MATERIALS
> 134yd (120m) / 2 balls Lana Grossa Maxi Tosca (55% wool, 45% acrylic, each approximately 1¾ oz [50g] and 102yd [92m]), in color 0068 / red-brown, 【4】 medium

OR

> 131yd (120m) / 1 skein Noro Iro (75% wool, 25% silk, each approximately 3½ oz [100g] and 131yd [120m]), in color 30 / gray-brown, 【5】 bulky
> One set of 5 size 8 (5mm) dpns, or size needed to obtain gauge
> Stitch marker

GAUGE

> 16 stitches and 30 rows = 4″ (10cm) in half-linen stitch, with lighter yarn
> 15 stitches and 28 rows = 4″ (10cm) in half-linen stitch, with heavier yarn

Gloves

The right and left are identical.

CUFF

Long-tail cast on 32 stitches.

Distribute stitches evenly over 4 dpns—8 stitches on each needle.

Join to work in the round, being careful not to twist cast-on edge. Place marker at the beginning of the round.

Work rounds in k1, p1 rib for 1″ (2.5cm), ending at marker.

Beginning with round 1, work half-linen stitch pattern as follows.

Round 1 *K1, wyif slip 1 purlwise; repeat from * to end.

Rounds 2 and 4 Knit.

Round 3 *Wyif slip 1 purlwise, k1; repeat from * to end.

Work 4-row half-linen stitch pattern until piece measures approximately 3″ (7.5cm). End after working round 3.

(Shorten or lengthen for finished length here.)

SHAPE WRIST

Decrease Round Skp in first 2 stitches of needles 1 and 3; k2tog in last 2 stitches of needles 2 and 4—7 stitches on each needle.

Begin with round 3 of stitch pattern.

Beginning with round 3 will maintain the continuity of the stitch pattern.

Work until piece measures approximately 4″ (10cm). End after working round 1 of stitch pattern.

HAND

First Increase (Knit) Round Work lifted increase into first stitch of needles 1 and 3 and into last stitch of needles 2 and 4—8 stitches on each needle.

Beginning with round 1 of stitch pattern, work 3 rounds even.

Beginning with round 1 will maintain the continuity of the stitch pattern.

Second Increase (Knit) Round Work lifted increase into first stitch of needle 1 and into last stitch of needle 4—9, 8, 8, 9 stitches on needles.

Sean's Fingerless Gloves

Beginning with round 3 of stitch pattern, work 3 rounds even.

Beginning with round 3 will maintain the continuity of the stitch pattern.

Repeat second increase round—10, 8, 8, 10 stitches on needles.

Working round 1 of stitch pattern, work to last 4 stitches on needle 4.

Put final 4 stitches of needle 4 and first 4 stitches of needle 1 onto a holder. Re-position marker here for new beginning of round.

Turn, and e-wrap cast on 4 stitches onto end of needle 4—6, 8, 8, 10 stitches on needles. Turn. Beginning with round 2, continue in stitch pattern.

Distribute stitches evenly over 4 dpns—8 on each needle.

Work even for 2½″ (6.5 cm), or to 1″ (2.5cm) short of desired length.

Work k1, p1 rib for 1″ (2.5cm).

Bind off in rib.

THUMB

Distribute 8 stitches from holder onto 2 needles.

With RS facing, pick up and knit 4 stitches along cast-on edge of thumb opening.

Work rounds in k1, p1 rib for 2″ (5cm).

Bind off in rib.

Skating Coat

DESIGNED BY SALLY

This piece is meant to have the vintage feel of an old-time skating coat. I was particularly happy with how the sleeves contributed. And I look forward to wearing it, with my new "boy" skates on the Rideau Canal some sunny winter day in Ottawa.

SKILL LEVEL
Experienced

SIZES
> S (M, L, 1X, 2X)
> Finished bust 40 (43, 46, 49, 52)" (101.5 [109, 117, 124.5, 132]cm)
> Finished hem 63 (67, 72, 76, 81)" (160 [170, 183, 193, 206]cm)
> Finished length 33 (33½, 34, 34½, 35)" (84 [85, 86, 87.5, 89]cm)
> Finished shoulder width 14½" (37cm)
> Finished waist length 15 (15½, 16, 16½, 17)" (38 [39.5, 40.5, 42, 43]cm)
> Finished sleeve length 30½ (31, 31½, 32, 32½)" (77.5 [79, 80, 81, 82.5]cm)

Model was made in size M.

MATERIALS
> 1720 (1910, 2100, 2290, 2480)yd (1550 [1720, 1890, 2060, 2230]m) / 4 (4, 5, 5, 6) skeins Cascade Eco+ (100% wool, each approximately 8¾ oz [250g] and 478yd [437m]), in color 8511 (dark red), (5) bulky
> One pair size 6 (4mm) needles
> One pair size 8 (5mm) needles, or size needed to obtain gauge
> One circular needle, size 6 (4mm), 40" (101.5cm) long
> Stitch holder
> 10 buttons, 1" (2.5cm) wide

GAUGE
> 16 stitches and 22 rows = 4" (10cm) in stockinette stitch, over larger needles
> 18–20 stitches and 22 rows = 4" (10cm) in 2x2 rib, over larger needles

PATTERN NOTES
1. The rib gauge is offered as a guide for the actual knitting, but it is a range because rib is stretchy. Because of this, a stockinette stitch gauge is a more accurate indication of how you should knit. Please take the time to work a stockinette stitch gauge swatch.
2. The buttons were handmade by Eileen Petre (www.souptoknits.etsy.com).

Coat

BACK

EDGING

With smaller needles, cable cast on 236 (254, 272, 290, 308) stitches.

RS Rows *K2, [p1, k1] 3 times, p1; repeat from * to last 2 stitches, k2.

✳ FLATTER & FIT ✳

Sleeve length is measured from center body to end of sleeve. For more information, see Glossary, page 167.

- If I were to change the pattern, it would be to make the skirt longer—by working more rows between the decreases. But I am not very tall, and I also knew as I was knitting that to make the skirt longer would have required another ball for this size, and another ball in the same dye lot was not available.
- If your row gauge does not match the pattern's, the length of the skirts and of the sleeves will be affected—because the garment's length is based on number of rows, not a measurement. Adjust accordingly (by changing the numbers of rows between decreases and increases).
- All width measurements (and the schematics) are based on the stockinette stitch gauge (which is the widest to which the garment could be stretched), but the rib will pull the garment up to 4" (10cm) narrower in the upper body. The waist will stretch out much wider than the gauge would suggest. And the hem will actually pleat itself to 20" (51cm) narrower the measurements indicate.
- This garment was felted very slightly—to make the fabric plumper and more coat-like, and to minimize stretching. (Instructions for this are in the finishing section.) Felting as directed will not change the width.
- All length measurements are for the garment as knit. After wearing—and even after felting slightly—it may stretch up to 2" (5cm) in length.
- The sleeve length seems long, but this allows for the blousing.

WS Rows *P2, [k1, p1] 3 times, k1; repeat from * to last 2 stitches, p2.
Beginning and ending with a RS row, work 5 rows.
Next Row (WS) *P2, k7; repeat from * to last 2 stitches, p2.
The back skirt has 26 (28, 30, 32, 34) rib panels.

SKIRT
Change to larger needles.
Work 2x7 rib for 8 rows.

✳ TECHNIQUE ✳

I believe it is standard to describe rib as the number of knit stitches followed by the number of purl stitches. This standard will be maintained through all following rib patterns.

**First Rib Decrease Row (RS) At beginning of first and all odd-numbered panels, k1, skp; otherwise work rib as established—223 (240, 257, 274, 291) stitches.

✳ TECHNIQUE ✳

1. A panel is a RS k2 plus any following purls.
2. All following decreases are set up so a RS knit—either at the beginning or end of a panel—overlaps a RS purl.
3. Unless working a decrease (or, later, an increase), work rib as established.

Work in 2x6 and 2x7 rib for 7 rows.
(Shorten or lengthen for finished length by working fewer or more rows between following decreases.)
Second Rib Decrease Row (RS) Work to purl stitch that ends second and all even-numbered panels, then k2tog, k1—210 (226, 242, 258, 274) stitches.
Work 2x6 rib for 7 rows.
Third Rib Decrease Row (RS) Work to purl stitch that ends first and all odd-numbered panels, then k2tog, k1—197 (212, 227, 242, 257) stitches.
Work 2x5 and 2x6 rib for 7 rows.
Fourth Rib Decrease Row (RS) At beginning of second and all even-numbered panels, k1, skp—184 (198, 212, 226, 240) stitches.
Work 2x5 rib for 7 rows.
Repeat First Rib Decrease Row—171 (184, 197, 210, 223) stitches.
Work 2x4 and 2x5 rib for 7 rows.
Repeat Second Rib Decrease Row—158 (170, 182, 194, 206) stitches.
Work 2x4 rib for 7 rows.
Repeat Third Rib Decrease Row—145 (156, 167, 178, 189) stitches.

Skating Coat

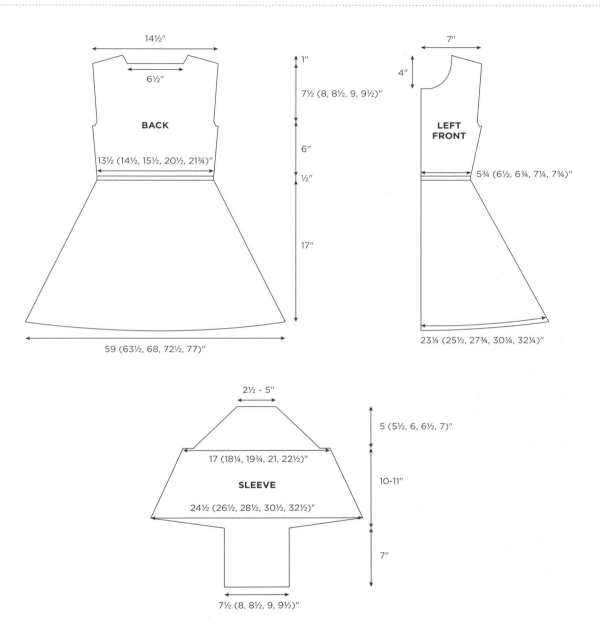

BACK

14½"

6½"

1"

7½ (8, 8½, 9, 9½)"

6"

½"

17"

13½ (14½, 15½, 20½, 21¾)"

59 (63½, 68, 72½, 77)"

LEFT FRONT

7"

4"

5¾ (6½, 6¾, 7¼, 7¾)"

23¼ (25½, 27¾, 30¼, 32¼)"

SLEEVE

2½ - 5"

5 (5½, 6, 6½, 7)"

17 (18¼, 19¾, 21, 22½)"

10-11"

24½ (26½, 28½, 30½, 32½)"

7"

7½ (8, 8½, 9, 9½)"

ALL MEASUREMENTS ARE BASED ON STOCKINETTE GAUGE.

Work 2x3 and 2x4 rib for 7 rows.
Repeat Fourth Rib Decrease Row—132 (142, 152, 162, 172) stitches.
Work 2x3 rib for 7 rows.
Repeat First Rib Decrease Row—119 (128, 137, 146, 155) stitches.
Work 2x2 and 2x3 rib for 7 rows.
Repeat Second Rib Decrease Row—106 (114, 122, 130, 138) stitches.
Work 2x2 rib for 7 rows.
Repeat Third Rib Decrease Row—93 (100, 107, 114, 121) stitches.**
Work 2x1 and 2x2 rib for 3 (3, 3, 5, 5) rows.
S (M, L) Sizes Only Repeat Fourth Rib Decrease Row—80 (86, 92) stitches.
Work 2x1 rib for 1 row. End after working a WS row.
All Sizes 80 (86, 92, 114, 121) stitches; piece measures approximately 17" (43cm).

REVERSE STOCKINETTE WAISTBAND
S (M, L) Sizes Only, Decrease Row (RS) With smaller needles, k2, *k2tog, k1; repeat from * to end—54 (58, 62) stitches.
1X (2X) Sizes Only, Decrease Row (RS) With smaller needles, k2, *k2tog, k2, k2tog, k1; repeat from * to end—82 (87) stitches.
All Sizes Knit 1 row, purl 1 (RS) row, then knit 1 row. With larger needles, knit 1 (RS) row.

UPPER BACK
S (M, L) Sizes Only, Increase Row (WS) P2, *[work lifted increase knitwise then purl] into next stitch, p1; repeat from * to end—80 (86, 92) stitches.
1X (2X) Sizes Only, Increase Row (WS) P2, *k1, p2, [work lifted increase knitwise then purl] into next stitch, p1; repeat from * to end—98 (104) stitches.
All Sizes Work 2x1 rib to 6" (15cm) above waistband.

✳ FLATTER & FIT ✳

The upper back is knit in 2x1 rib, and the upper front is knit in 2x2 rib. This is done to flatter and fit the female form.

End after working a WS row.
(Shorten or lengthen for waist length here.)

SHAPE ARMHOLE
Bind off 2 (4, 6, 8, 10) stitches at beginning of next 2 rows—76 (78, 80, 82, 84) stitches.
Decrease Row (RS) K2, skp, work rib as established to last 4 stitches, k2tog, k2.
Work 1 WS row in 2x1 rib as established.
Repeat the last 2 rows 8 (9, 10, 11, 12) times more—58 stitches.
Work rib as established until armhole measures 7 ½ (8, 8 ½, 9, 9 ½)" (19 [20.5, 21.5, 23, 24]cm). End after working a WS row.

SHAPE RIGHT SHOULDER AND BACK NECK
Maintain rib as established through all following shaping.
Bind off 4 stitches at beginning of next RS row. Work to 14 stitches on right needle. Put remaining stitches onto holder. Turn.
*Bind off 1 stitch at neck edge twice, and 4 stitches at armhole edge 3 times—0 stitches.

SHAPE LEFT SHOULDER AND BACK NECK
Return to remaining stitches, RS facing.
Next Row (RS) Bind off 22 stitches (for Back neck), then work to end—18 stitches.
Bind off 4 stitches at beginning of next WS row.
Work as Shape Right Shoulder and Back Next from * to end.

LEFT FRONT
EDGING
With smaller needles, cable cast on 93 (102, 111, 120, 129) stitches.
RS Rows *K2, [p1, k1] 3 times, p1; repeat from * to last 3 stitches, k3.
WS Rows P3, *[k1, p1] 3 times, k1, p2; repeat from *.
Beginning and ending with a RS row, work 5 rows.
Next Row (WS) P3, *k7, p2; repeat from *.

SKIRT
Change to larger needles.
With a stockinette stitch at the front edge, work 2x7 rib for 8 rows.
The Left Front skirt has 10 (11, 12, 13, 14) rib panels.
Work as Back Skirt from ** to ** but with different numbers of stitches each time. End after working a third Decrease Row—38 (41, 45, 48, 52) stitches.
You will have decreased by 10 (11, 12, 13, 14) stitches

after every alternate decrease.
Work 2x1 and 2x2 rib for 3 rows.
Repeat fourth rib Decrease Row—33 (36, 39, 42, 45) stitches.
Work 2x1 rib for 1 row. End after working a WS row.

REVERSE STOCKINETTE WAISTBAND
Decrease Row (RS) With smaller needles, k2, *k2tog, k1; repeat from * to last 4 stitches, k2tog, k2—23 (25, 27, 29, 31) stitches.
Knit 1 row, purl 1 (RS) row, then knit 1 row.
With larger needles, knit 1 (RS) row.

UPPER FRONT
Increase Row (WS) P3, *[work lifted increase knitwise then purl] into next stitch, p1; repeat from * to end—33 (36, 39, 42, 45) stitches.
With an extra stockinette stitch at the front edge, work as follows.
***Work 2x1 rib for 6 rows.
Increase Row (RS) Work lifted increase in purl stitches of first and all odd-numbered panels—38 (42, 45, 49, 52) stitches.
Work 2x2 and 2x1 rib for 5 rows.
Increase Row (RS) Work lifted increase in purl stitches of second and all even-numbered panels—43 (47, 51, 55, 59) stitches.
Work 2x2 rib until piece measures same length as Back above waistband.***
End after working a WS row.

SHAPE ARMHOLE
Bind off 2 (4, 6, 8, 10) stitches at beginning of next RS row—41 (43, 45, 47, 49) stitches.
All WS Rows Work rib as established, but begin and end with p3.
All RS Rows Choose between following Decrease Rows: otherwise, work rib as established.
Single Decrease Row (RS) When row starts with 4 or 5 knit stitches, k2, skp.
Double Decrease Row (RS) When row starts with 3 knit stitches followed by 2 purls, k2, sk2p.
Repeat RS Decrease Row—28 stitches.
Work rib as established until armhole measures 4½ (5, 5½, 6, 6½)" (11.5 [12.5, 14, 15, 16.5]cm). End after working a RS row.

SHAPE NECK AND SHOULDER

Maintain rib as established through all following shaping.

At neck edge, bind off 2 stitches twice and 1 stitch 4 times. AT THE SAME TIME, when armhole measures same length as Back, bind off 5 stitches at armhole edge 4 times.

Bind off tightly for a narrow shoulder, more loosely for a flexible shoulder.

RIGHT FRONT

EDGING

With smaller needles, cable cast on 93 (102, 111, 120, 129) stitches.

RS Rows K3, *[p1, k1] 3 times, p1, k2; repeat from * to end.

WS Rows *P2, [k1, p1] 3 times, k1; repeat from * to last 3 stitches, p3.

Beginning and ending with a RS row, work 5 rows.

Next Row (WS) *P2, k7; repeat from * to last 3 stitches, p3.

SKIRT

Change to larger needles.

With an extra stockinette stitch at the front edge, work 2x7 rib for 8 rows.

The Right Front skirt has 10 (11, 12, 13, 14) rib panels.

Work as Back Skirt from ** to ** but with different numbers of stitches each time. End after working a third Decrease Row—38 (41, 45, 48, 52) stitches.

You will have decreased by 10 (11, 12, 13, 14) stitches after every alternate decrease.

Work 2x1 and 2x2 rib for 3 rows.

Repeat fourth rib Decrease Row—33 (36, 39, 42, 45) stitches.

Work 2x1 rib for 1 row. End after working a WS row.

REVERSE STOCKINETTE WAISTBAND

Decrease Row (RS) With smaller needles, k3, *k2tog, k1; repeat from * to end—23 (25, 27, 29, 31) stitches.

Knit 1 row, purl 1 (RS) row, then knit 1 row.

With larger needles, knit 1 (RS) row.

UPPER FRONT

Increase Row (WS) *P1, [work lifted increase knitwise then purl] into next stitch; repeat from * to last 3 stitches, p3—33 (36, 39, 42, 45) stitches.

With an extra stockinette stitch at the front edge, work as Left Front, Upper Front from *** to ***.

End after working a RS row.

SHAPE ARMHOLE

Bind off 2 (4, 6, 8, 10) stitches at beginning of next WS row—41 (43, 45, 47, 49) stitches.

All WS Rows Work rib as established, but begin and end with p3.

All RS Rows Choose between following Decrease Rows: otherwise, work rib as established.

Single Decrease Row (RS) When row ends with 4 or 5 knit stitches, in last 4 stitches, k2tog, k2.

Double Decrease Row (RS) When row ends with 2 purl stitches followed by 3 knits, in last 5 stitches, k3tog, k2.

Repeat RS Decrease Row—28 stitches.

Work rib as established until armhole measures same as Left Front. End after working a WS row.

SHAPE NECK AND SHOULDER

Work as Left Front, Shape Neck and Shoulder.

SLEEVES

CUFF

With smaller needles, cable cast on 39 (41, 45, 47, 51) stitches.

Beginning and ending all RS rows with k1 and all WS rows with p1, work 1x1 rib to 7" (18cm).

(Shorten for sleeve here.)

End after working a WS row.

Next Row Knit, decreasing 1 (0, 1, 0, 1) stitch—38 (41, 44, 47, 50) stitches.

LOWER SLEEVE

Change to larger needles.

Next Row (WS) *P2, k1; repeat from * to last 2 stitches, p2.

Work 2x1 rib for 1 row.

✳ FLATTER & FIT ✳

The only schematic measurement not based upon the stockinette stitch gauge is the cuff of the sleeve. Because this cuff is long, it will hold the rib gauge.

First Rib Increase Row (WS) M1 (knitwise) before first knit stitch of each panel—50 (54, 58, 62, 66) stitches.

The Sleeve has 12 (13, 14, 15, 16) panels.

Work 2x2 rib for 1 row.

Second Rib Increase Row (WS) M1 (knitwise) after final knit stitch of each panel—62 (67, 72, 77, 82) stitches.

Work 2x3 rib for 1 RS row.

Repeat First Rib Increase Row—74 (80, 86, 92, 98) stitches.

Work 2x4 rib for 1 RS row.

Repeat Second Rib Increase Row—86 (93, 100, 107, 114) stitches.

Work 2x5 rib for 1 RS row.

Repeat First Rib Increase Row—98 (106, 114, 122, 130) stitches.

Work 2x6 rib for 2 (4, 6, 8, 10) rows.
(Lengthen for sleeve here.)

End after working a WS row.

REVERSE STOCKINETTE BORDER

With smaller needles, knit 2 rows, purl 1 (RS) row, knit 1 row.

With larger needles, knit 1 (RS) row.

UPPER SLEEVE

Next Row (WS) *P2, k6; repeat from * to last 2 stitches, p2.

Work 2x6 rib for 6 rows.

First Rib Decrease Row (RS) At beginning of first and all odd-numbered panels, k1, skp—92 (99, 107, 114, 122) stitches.

Work 2x5 and 2x6 rib for 7 rows.

Second Rib Decrease Row (RS) Work to purl stitch that ends second and all even-numbered panels, then k2tog, k1—86 (93, 100, 107, 114) stitches.

Work 2x5 rib for 7 rows.

Third Rib Decrease Row (RS) Work to purl stitch that ends first and all odd-numbered panels, then k2tog, k1—80 (86, 93, 99, 106) stitches.

Work 2x4 and 2x5 rib for 7 rows.

Fourth Rib Decrease Row (RS) At beginning of second and all even-numbered panels, k1, skp—74 (80, 86, 92, 98) stitches.

Work 2x4 rib for 7 rows.

Repeat First Rib Decrease Row—68 (73, 79, 84, 90) stitches.

Work 2x3 and 2x4 rib for 1 row.

Sleeve measures approximately 17–18" (43–46cm), stretched.

SHAPE CAP

Maintain rib as established through all following shaping.

Bind off 2 (4, 6, 8, 10) stitches at beginning of next 2 rows—64 (65, 67, 68, 70) stitches.

The sleeve now has 12 (11, 12, 11, 12) panels, but this will change very quickly as cap decreases are made.

Cap Decrease Row (RS) K1, skp, work to last 3 stitches, k2tog, k1.

Work 1 WS row.

Repeat the last 2 rows once more.

First Cap + Rib Decrease Row (RS) Work cap decrease, AT THE SAME TIME decrease 1 purl stitch in all even-numbered panels.

Look below cap shaping to see which are the odd-numbered and which are the even-numbered panels.

When rib decrease combines with cap decrease at beginning of row, k1, s2kp.

When rib decrease combines with cap decrease at end of row, in last 4 stitches, k3tog, k1.

Work 2x3 rib for 1 WS row.

Repeat cap Decrease Row 3 times more. End after working a WS row.

Second Cap + Rib Decrease Row (RS) Work cap decrease, AT THE SAME TIME decrease 1 purl stitch in all odd-numbered panels.

Work 2x2 and 2x3 rib for 1 WS row.

Repeat Cap Decrease Row 3 times more. End after working a WS row.

Repeat First Cap + Rib Decrease Row.

Work 2x2 rib for 1 WS row.

Repeat Cap Decrease Row.

Work 1 WS row.

Repeat Second Cap + Rib Decrease Row.

Work 2x1 and 2x2 rib for 1 WS row.

Repeat Cap Decrease Row.

Work 1 WS row.

Bind Off + Rib Decrease Row (RS) Bind off 2 stitches, then repeat Second Cap + Rib Decrease Row.

Bind off 2 stitches at beginning of next WS row, then bind off remaining stitches.

Because panels disappear, it is difficult to give a final stitch count. Depending upon your size, you should have 10–20 stitches remaining. Because it is rib, it doesn't matter what the final stitch count is.

FINISHING

NECK EDGING

Sew shoulder seams, sewing 4 stitches of Back shoulder bind-offs to 5 stitches of Front shoulder bind-offs.

With smaller needles and RS facing, pick up and knit around neck edge as follows:

- 1 stitch for every bound-off stitch around shaping of Front and Back neck
- 1 stitch for every 2-row step between bound-off stitches
- 3 stitches for every 4 rows (along straight edges)
- 3 stitches for every 4 bound-off stitches across Back neck bound-off edge

—approximately 61 stitches.

On the next row, increase or decrease evenly (as needed) to achieve 61 stitches.

Knit 1 (WS) row, purl 1 row, then knit 2 rows.

HOOD

Next Row (WS) P3, *k1, p2; repeat from * to last 4 stitches, p1, k3.

With an extra stockinette stitch at each front edge, work 2x1 rib for 7 rows.

Increase Row (RS) M1 (knitwise) before first (WS) knit stitch of each panel, otherwise work as established—80 stitches.

Change to larger needles.

Work in 2x2 rib to 13½" (34.5cm) above neck edging.

End after working a WS row.

Next (Short) Row (RS) Work 36 stitches. Turn.

Next Row Sl 1, work to end.

Slip all stitches purlwise and with yarn to WS.

Continue working short rows over RS rows, leaving 4 stitches behind each time to 20 stitches left after working a WS row. Cut yarn.

Return to 40 stitches at other side of hood, and work 1 RS row.

Next (Short) Row (WS) Work 36 stitches. Turn.

Next Row Sl 1, work to end.

Continue working short rows over WS rows, leaving 4 stitches behind each time to 20 stitches left after working a RS row. Cut yarn.

With RS together, 3-needle bind-off two sides of hood together. Turn hood to RS.

FRONT AND HOOD EDGINGS

With long circular needle and RS facing, pick up and knit around entire Front and hood edge as follows: 2 stitches for 3 rows over areas worked on smaller needles, 5 stitches for 7 rows over areas worked on larger needles.

Knit 1 (WS) row, then purl 1 row, then knit 1 row.

Next Row (RS) Knit, binding off all stitches around edge of hood.

Leave stitches of Right Front at end of long circular needle.

LEFT FRONT EDGING

Work up Left Front edge (ending at hood bind-off) as follows.

****Increase Row (WS)** P2, *[k1, p1] 3 times, M1 (knitwise), p1; repeat from *, ending with k1, p2.

Eliminate final increases that would have you not end with p2.

Beginning and ending all RS rows with k2 and all WS rows with p2, work 1x1 rib to 4" (10cm). Bind off.

Mark places in purl stitches of Left Front edging for 5 evenly spaced buttons, beginning 1" (2.5cm) below neck and ending 8–9" (20.5–23cm) below waistband.

✳ TECHNIQUE ✳

Space buttons evenly on either side of waistband, or place a button at the waistband and space evenly from it.

RIGHT FRONT EDGING

Return to stitches of Right Front, WS facing. Work down Right Front from hood bind-off as Left Front Edging from **** until 1x1 rib measures 3" (7.5cm). End after working a WS row.

Next Row, Begin Buttonholes Continue with 1x1 rib as established to places for buttonholes, ending after working p1; [skp, yo] at each buttonhole.

Next Row, Continue Buttonholes Work 1x1 rib, knitting yo's to not twist them.

Next Row, Finish Buttonholes Work 1x1 rib to each buttonhole, purl through buttonhole itself, then drop purl stitch from left needle.

Continue with 1x1 rib until Right Front edging measures same as Left Front edging. Bind off.

Sew Sleeves into armholes.

Sew Sleeve and side seams.

Sew buttons to Left Front edging to match placement of buttonholes.

Sew 5 buttons to Right Front edging that match buttonholes (for doubled-breasted effect).

FELTING (OPTIONAL)

✳ TECHNIQUE ✳

Slightly felting as directed will give the garment the feeling of a coat rather than a sweater. But do this *very carefully* and as directed. It would be prudent to practice on a swatch first. And if using a substitute yarn, you would definitely need to experiment with a swatch.

Read about felting and size in the Fit section below the measurements.

Wash as directed in a wool-wash solution. Tumble the garment on a no-heat dryer setting (It is essential that the dryer have no heat!) with towels *for a few moments only. Do not leave unattended*: check frequently until fabric is plumped slightly. Dry flat to finish.

CHAPTER FOUR

Feeling Festive

Bread and wine . . . dinner and a movie . . . love and marriage . . . knitting and Christmas. They are natural, traditional, obvious, and wonderful pairings. And while much of this book speaks to this pairing—we could knit Christmas sweaters for the kids, we often knit Christmas gifts, and we knit to keep warm through the holidays—this chapter is dedicated to the decorative traditions of Christmas.

First, the tree ornaments. We start with a pair of ornaments that young and/ or old hands could make, move on to ornaments specifically for the knitters among us, and end with traditional pieces. Then there is a pair of stockings— one very traditional and one not. And finally, the big item: a Christmas tree skirt.

Some of these pieces might take less than an hour; some could take weeks. You might want to make a plan to determine how much you can reasonably do . . . because it's difficult to think about Christmas without remembering the snarl of time management we can get into.

I, personally, am not one of those who prepares for Christmas particularly early. In truth, I'm one of the apparent majority who start Christmas preparations in early December and finish by the 21st. This has always served me well enough.

But one year I stepped out of character and start- ed early. I don't remember exactly what precipitated this. Perhaps it was that I would have more guests than usual over a longer-than-usual Christmas period. Whatever the particulars, it promised to be a heady and busy time, so I started *really* early. I think I was absolutely finished by the first week in December. So what did I do? I extended my list of people for whom I wished to make gifts, and I started all over again. It was my busiest Christmas ever!

Whatever your character, perhaps this is not the best time to step out of it. If you normally start early, then do so; if you normally hold off until the spirit moves you, then do so. Truly, no one wants you to stress yourself: they're happier being around you if you're happy within yourself.

And if you over-extend yourself, please be kind. See this as a testament to your love of knitting *and* to the spirit of giving, then bless yourself.　**—SALLY**

Easy Open Heart

DESIGNED BY SALLY

When I was artist-in-residence at a folk art museum, I did a day of Christmas ornaments for children over six. The kids were so thrilled with this easily mastered little piece that they took every scrap of yarn I had to make as many as they could on our day together. It was a wonderful experience, and I hope you have a young one to share it with.

SKILL LEVEL
Beginner

SIZE
All measurements are approximate.
> Width 3" (7.5cm)
> Height 3" (7.5cm)

MATERIALS
> 5yd (4.5m) 100% wool, in color red, (4) medium
> 10" (25.5cm) wire, 20-gauge
> Two dpns, size 6 (4mm)
> *Optional* 14" (35.5cm) wired ribbon, ¾–1" (2–2.5cm) wide, any color

GAUGE
Gauge does not matter.

Heart

Cast on 2 stitches.
Row 1 Kf&b twice—4 stitches.

✳ TECHNIQUE ✳
If you are new to knitting, just cast on 4 stitches.

All Rows Without turning work, slide stitches back to other end of needle, k4.
You are making I-cord.
Continue until piece measures 9" (23cm).
Final Row Slip 1, k2tog, pass slip stitch over final 2 stitches.

INSPIRATION

This piece was designed so even those who don't yet knit (your nearest and dearest six-year old) can make it. I-cord is pretty easy to teach. And neat, even tension is hardly important, since this piece will be very much shrunk.

Cut yarn, and draw yarn through final 2 stitches.

✳ TECHNIQUE ✳
If you are teaching someone new to knitting, just draw your cut yarn through the final 4 stitches.

Sew in both tails.

✳ TECHNIQUE ✳
Always sew in tails before felting your piece. Otherwise, they may become matted messes.

ASSEMBLY

Felt by washing I-cord in hot water with cold rinse. Let dry, or tumble dry in hot dryer.

Fold one end of wire back ½" (13mm).

Thread folded end of wire through I-cord.

Cut wire ½" (13mm) longer than I-cord, then fold final end of wire back into I-cord (to bury it).

Form a circle with ends of wire and I-cord overlapping.

Thread 20" (51cm) piece of yarn onto tapestry needle.

Leaving a 4" (10cm) tail, push needle straight through overlapped ends.

Wrap remaining yarn around this join until it is well covered and secure. Leave a 4" (10cm) tail.

With both tails, tie a square knot at the join.

With an overhand knot, use what remains of the tails to form a 3" (7.5cm) hanger.

Trim tails above overhand knot.

Bend wire to form a heart shape.

Optional (Not Shown) Tie ribbon in a bow around the heart, to one side of center and to cover the join.

Trim ends of ribbon to suit.

Mini Evergreen Wreath and UFO Ornament

DESIGNED BY SALLY

I used to make an ornament every year—for special people to whom I wanted to give a little more than just a card. The Mini Evergreen Wreath was the first ornament I made to suit this purpose. And while it might seem complex, I've taught it to young children. All you need know how to do is knit I-cord (for which directions are given) and tie knots.

The UFO ornament is for those knitters surrounded by Un-Finished Objects! (Sometimes our families don't understand this, but we knitters do.) It could also be the promise of a sweater we can't quite finish before the event.

By the way, the UFO ornament began as a corsage—with a pin rather than a hanger—made as gifts for the fabulous knitters who won awards at my Kitchener-Waterloo Knitters' Guild's semi-annual adjudicated show.

Mini Evergreen Wreath

SKILL LEVEL
Beginner

SIZE
All measurements are approximate.
> Width 3" (7.5cm)
> Height 3" (7.5cm)

MATERIALS
> 9yd (8.2m) yarn, in color brown, (**4**) medium
> Two dpns, size 8 (5mm)
> 3yd (2.7mm) yarns, in 3 different greens, (**3**) or (**4**) light to medium
> 48 beads, any color
> Glue
> *Optional* 12" (30.5cm) ribbon, ¼" (6mm) wide, any color

GAUGE
Gauge does not matter

I-CORD PIECES (MAKE 3)
With brown yarn, and leaving 8" (20.5cm) tail, cast on 3 stitches.
All Rows K3. Without turning work, slide stitches back to other end of needle.
You are making I-cord.
Continue until piece measures 7" (18cm).

INSPIRATION

If you are, or are teaching, a new knitter, don't worry about a neat, even gauge: the three pieces of I-cord will be covered by greenery.

Last Row K3tog.

Cut yarn, leaving 8" (20.5cm) tail. Pull tail through last stitch.

ASSEMBLY

FORM WREATH

With an overhead knot, tie 3 I-cord tails together as close as possible to I-cords.

Braid I-cords, stretching as needed so all three meet at the end.

Don't braid too tightly or too loosely. You want the I-cords to cross 18 to 20 times.

It will be difficult to keep the end of the braid tight.

Don't worry: this space may be filled with ribbon.

With an overhand knot, tie remaining tails as close as possible to end of braid.

With a square knot, tie tails from both ends together, and as tightly as possible, to make a circle (which becomes the wreath).

With an overhand knot, tie all tails to form a 3" (7.5cm) loop to serve as hanger.

Trim tails.

ADD GREENERY

Wrap each 3yd (2.7m) length of green yarn around 3 fingers 24 times. Cut at the bottom.

This makes strands approximately 4" (10cm) long.
*Choose 2 strands of one color and 1 strand in each of the other two colors, then tie the 4 strands around a space in the braid; trim ends to ½" (13mm). Repeat from * until all braid spaces have been filled. Fill any bare spots with remaining strands.

DECORATE
Place a drop of glue on a greenery knot.
Place 2 to 3 beads to cover the glue, and gently press the beads into the wreath.
Continue around the wreath, covering all greenery knots with a cluster of beads. Let dry.
Optional (Not Shown) Tie the ribbon into a bow around the top of the wreath; trim tails to suit.

UFO Ornament

SKILL LEVEL
Beginner

SIZE
All measurements are approximate.
> Width 3½" (9cm)
> Height 5" (12.5cm)

MATERIALS
> 6yd (5.5m) yarn, any color, **3** or **4** light or medium
> One pair size 5 (3.75mm) needles
> One dpn, size 0 (2mm) or smaller

> 2 toothpicks
> 2 beads (that fit onto ends of toothpicks)
> 8" (20.5cm) wired ribbon, 1½" (4cm) wide, in color to match yarn and to be used as pants
> *Optional* Craft glue

GAUGE
Gauge does not matter.

Cast on 12 stitches.
Knit every row until piece measures 1" (2.5cm).
Cast on 5 stitches at beginning of next 2 rows (for sleeves)—22 stitches.
Knit every row to just less than ½" (13mm) from sleeve cast-on.
Knit next row onto dpn.
Cut sharp points off one end of each of the toothpicks, and attach a bead to each cut end.
Optional Use glue if the seal is not tight.
Final Row Onto one toothpick, knit to middle of row; cut yarn to 24" (61cm).
Beginning at opposite end of dpn, slip remaining stitches onto second toothpick.

FINISHING
Wind remaining yarn into a small, tight ball.
Gently push points of each toothpick through the ball.
Thread 8" (20.5cm) yarn onto a tapestry needle, and take it through the top of the sweater.
Be sure you have found the ornament's center of gravity.
With an overhand knot, tie both ends to make a loop that serves as hanger.
Fold ribbon in half—to look like a pair of pants.
If the ribbon is not reversible, cut it in half so RS is to the front.
Sew upper edges of ribbon to WS of sweater.
Trim lower edges of ribbon to suit.
If you use pinking shears, they make a better lower edge. If not, you might want to seal the lower edge with nail polish or a commercial product.

INSPIRATION

When I taught young children to do the Heart and Wreath ornaments, they learned I-cord on a knitting machine—and all left wanted a knitting machine for Christmas! If you have a machine, a young child can be taught to make I-cord. Or the child can learn to do this by hand. Or the cords can be made on a spool knitter. There are lots of ways to teach young hands to knit!

Leftover-Sock-Yarn Stocking

DESIGNED BY SALLY

Entrelac is a fascinating technique. It was the first "modular" knitting technique I learned, and I think I did nothing else for three years! If you have never done it, you might find it equally addictive.

And then there's that other addiction: sock knitting! I designed this stocking for those of us who have great amounts of variously colored, leftover sock yarn.

SKILL LEVEL
Intermediate

SIZE
All measurements are approximate.

> Circumference 13″ (33cm)
> Height of leg (above top of heel, with cuff turned back) 11″ (28cm)

MATERIALS
> Approximately 500yd (450m) sock yarn, in full or part balls and in any number of colors, [1] super-fine
> One size 5 (3.75mm) circular needle, 16″ (40.5cm)
> One set of 5 dpns, size 5 (3.75mm)
> One size E-4 (3.5mm) crochet hook (or size close to this)
> Stitch marker

GAUGE
Two entrelac rectangles = approximately 4½″ (11.5cm) square
Gauge does not matter.

PATTERN NOTES
1. The stocking is worked from bottom to top. Toe, heel, and cuff are worked after the foot and leg are complete.
2. I used 3 colors of patterned sock yarn: A (red), B (red-purple), and C (purple). The foot was worked in doubled A (to the end of 2 sets of rectangles), then A + B (for 3 sets of rectangles), then doubled

B (for 3 sets of rectangles), then B + C (for 3 sets of rectangles), then finished with doubled C. The toe was worked in doubled A; the heel was worked in doubled B. The cuff lining was work in doubled C; the cuff outside was worked in B + C, then doubled B, then B + A, then doubled A.

Stocking

FOOT

FIRST OPEN RIGHT-LEANING TRIANGLES

Use doubled sock yarn throughout.

❋ TECHNIQUE ❋

An "open" triangle is one from which live stitches remain along the long edge: a "closed" rectangle—which appears later—is one in which there are no live stitches along the long edge.

With circular needle, long-tail cast on 48 stitches. Turn (so purl side of cast-on is facing).
Through the pattern, the stockinette stitch side will be described as the RS: the lean of the triangles and rectangles is determined from the stockinette stitch side. When done, you may decide (as I did) to turn the stocking inside out (with the purl side of the entrelac facing): the finishing directions will allow for either possibility.
Row 1 (WS) Slip 1 purlwise. Turn.
Always slip purlwise and with yarn to WS. Following directions will read "sl 1."
Row 2 K1. Turn.
Row 3 Sl 1, p1. Turn.
Row 4 K2. Turn.
Row 5 Sl 1, p2. Turn.
Row 6 K3. Turn.
WS Rows 7 (9, 11, 13, 15) Sl 1, p 3 (4, 5, 6, 7). Turn.
RS Rows 8 (10, 12, 14) K4 (5, 6, 7). Turn.
After Row 15, one 8-stitch triangle is formed and purl side is facing.
Repeat rows 1–15 five times more—6 triangles. End after working a purl row.
With purl side facing, join to form a circle, being careful not to twist triangles around the needle.
The needle will seem to be too long for the circle, but just let the extra cable protrude between the triangles.

FIRST LEFT-LEANING RECTANGLES

Beginning at cast-on tail, pick up and p8 along slip-stitch edge of first triangle. Turn.

Always pick up and knit in the back (purl) side of the slip stitches. The last stitch you purl into may be the first stitch on the left needle. If so, purl into this stitch but do not remove the original stitch from the left needle.
Next 8 RS Rows Sl 1, k6, skp (to join final stitch to next triangle). Turn.
Next 7 WS Rows Sl 1, p7. Turn.
End with RS row and after all 8 stitches of triangle have been absorbed.
***Next (RS) Row** Without turning work, pick up and k8 along slip-stitch edge of adjacent triangle. Turn.
Work 8 WS and 8 RS rows as above. End after working a knit row and after all stitches of triangle have been absorbed.
Repeat from * 4 times more—1 set of 6 Left-Leaning Rectangles is made. End after working knit row.

RIGHT-LEANING RECTANGLES

Without turning work, pick up and k8 along slip-stitch edge of adjacent rectangle. Turn.
Next 8 WS Rows Sl 1, p6, p2tog (to join final stitch to next rectangle). Turn.
Next 7 RS Rows Sl 1, k7. Turn.
End after working a purl row and after all stitches of rectangle have been absorbed.
****Next Row** Without turning work, pick up and p8 along slip-stitch edge of adjacent rectangle. Turn.
Work 8 RS and 8 WS rows of Right-Leaning Rectangles. End after working a purl row and after all stitches of rectangle have been absorbed.
Repeat from ** 4 times more—1 set of 6 Right-Leaning Rectangles is made. End after working a purl row.

LEFT-LEANING RECTANGLES

Without turning work, pick up and p8 along slip-stitch edge of adjacent rectangle. Turn.
Next 8 RS Rows Sl 1, k6, skp (to join final stitch to next rectangle). Turn.
Next 7 WS Rows Sl 1, P7. Turn.
End after working a knit row and after all stitches of rectangle have been absorbed.
*****Next Row** Without turning work, pick up and k8 along slip-stitch edge of adjacent rectangle. Turn.
Work 8 WS and 8 RS rows of Left-Leaning Rectangles. End after working a knit row and after all stitches of rectangle have been absorbed.
Repeat from *** 4 times more—1 set of 6 Left-Leaning Rectangles is made. End after working a knit row.

NEXT 2 SETS OF RECTANGLES
Work 1 set of 6 Right-Leaning Rectangles.
Work 1 set of 6 Left-Leaning Rectangles.

HEEL SPACE
Work 3 Right-Leaning Rectangles, then make a heel opening by making triangles (instead of rectangles) as follows.

CLOSED RIGHT-LEANING TRIANGLES
Without turning work, pick up and p8 along slip-stitch edge of adjacent rectangle. Turn.
****Row 2 (RS) Sl 1, k7. Turn.
Row 3 (WS) Sl 1, p1, psso, p5, p2tog. Turn.
Row 4 Sl 1, k6. Turn.
Row 5 Sl 1, p1, psso, p4, p2tog. Turn.
Continue in this manner, with bind-off at beginning of purl rows and p2tog at end of purl rows, and with 1 fewer stitch each knit row, until 2 stitches remain on each needle at end of a purl row. Turn.
Next Row (RS) Sl 1, k1. Turn.
Next Row (WS) Sl 1, p2tog, psso. Without turning work, slip last stitch from right needle onto left, p2tog. Without turning work, pick up and p1 along slip-stitch edge of adjacent rectangle, bind off 1, continue to pick up and purl along slip-stitch edge of adjacent rectangle to 8 stitches on right needle.
Turn, repeat from **** twice to form 2 more triangles; end with p2tog and 1 stitch on right needle. Do not turn work.

OPEN RIGHT-LEANING TRIANGLES
With purl side facing, slip remaining stitch onto left needle; loosely, and with knitted cast-on method, cast on 22 stitches—23 stitches on left needle. Turn.
With knit side facing (and to attach cast-on stitches), pick up and k1 in the corner (at the beginning of first Closed Right-Leaning Triangle)—24 stitches on right needle. Turn.
Work as rows 1–15 of First Open Right-Leaning Triangles (at the beginning of the pattern) until three 8-stitch triangles are formed. End after working a purl row.

LEG
Work 1 set of 6 Left-Leaning Rectangles.
The first 3 rectangles will join to the 3 Open Right-Leaning Triangles; the final 3 rectangles will join to Right-Leaning Rectangles as usual.
Continue with sets of Right-Leaning and Left-Leaning Rectangles, to 3 sets of each (or to desired height).

Leftover-Sock-Yarn Stocking

13"

11"

7"

End with a set of Left-Leaning Rectangles and after working a knit row.

CLOSED RIGHT-LEANING TRIANGLES
Without turning work, pick up and k8 along slip-stitch edge of adjacent rectangle.
Work as Closed Right-Leaning Triangles, beginning with row 3 after ****. Work until 6 Right-Leaning Triangles are made and 1 stitch remains on right needle.
Cut yarn, and draw through remaining stitch.

TOE
With knit side of entrelac facing, and using dpns, begin at start of cast-on edge of foot to pick up and knit in cast-on stitches as follows: *pick up and k3, yo; repeat from * around—64 stitches, 16 stitches on each needle.
Knit 1 round, knitting in back of all yos.
Knit 1 more round.
Knit 16 stitches of next round: this needle is now needle 4.
Place marker to indicate beginning of round.

✳ TECHNIQUE ✳

This is not how an anatomically correct toe would be made, but it will make the stocking hang nicely.

1st Decrease Round Over first 3 stitches of needles 1 and 3, k1, skp; over last 3 stitches of needles 2 and 4, k2tog, k1—1 stitch reduced on each needle.

2nd Decrease Round Over each needle, k1, skp, work to last 3 stitches, k2tog, k1—2 stitches reduced on each needle.

Repeat the last 2 rounds 3 times more—4 stitches on each needle.

Put stitches of needle 2 onto needle 1 and stitches of needle 4 onto needle 3. With knit side facing, graft stitches from each needle together.

HEEL

With knit side of entrelac facing, and using dpns, begin at a corner of the heel to pick up and knit in cast-on and bound-off stitches as follows: *pick up and k3, yo; repeat from * to end—64 stitches, 16 stitches on each needle.

Knit 1 round, knitting in back of all yo's.

Place marker to denote beginning of round.

Decrease Round Over first 3 stitches of needles 1 and 3, k1, skp; over last 3 stitches of needles 2 and 4, k2tog, k1.

Knit 1 round even.

Repeat the last 2 rounds 7 times more—8 stitches on each needle.

Put stitches of needle 2 onto needle 1 and stitches of needle 4 onto needle 3. With knit side facing, graft stitches from each needle together.

CUFF

LINING

With whichever you choose as RS facing, and using circular needle, begin at center back of stocking to pick up and knit in bound-off stitches as follows: *pick up and k2, yo; repeat from * to end—72 stitches.

Place marker to indicate beginning of rounds.

Knit 1 round, knitting in back of all yo's.

Continue to knit in rounds to 2½" (6.5cm). End at marker.

The cuff folds over to the RS, and the natural fold line of the cuff is at ½" (13mm) from the end of this lining.

OUTSIDE

If changing colors of doubled sock yarn, do so between first and second purl rounds.

Purl 2 rounds.

Knit 4 rounds.

Repeat the last 6 rounds two or three times more.

Bind off.

Turn cuff over at its natural fold line.

Whichever side you have chosen as the RS of the piece, the RSS side of the cuff is its RS.

FINISHING

Cut a 60" (152.5cm) piece of yarn.

Fold the piece in half. Make a slip knot at the fold, and place it onto the crochet hook. With the crochet hook, crochet a chain with doubled yarn to 5" (12.5cm). Draw tails through final loop.

Attach both ends of the hanger ½" (13mm) below the top of the folded cuff and at center back.

Block or steam-press.

❄ INSPIRATION

This stocking is made with a rather "quiet" color change. But many of us have a riot of leftover patterned sock yarn, so other possibilities abound! Here are two.

1. Use 2 balls, each with random lengths of patterned sock yarns knotted together. Be surprised!

2. Use one full ball of sock yarn (patterned or not) combined with one ball of random lengths of patterned sock yarn knotted together (perhaps moving from dark to light).

Alternatively, you can knit this stocking to gauge with singled Noro Silk Garden (and will use half as much yarn).

To see the latter two possibilities, go to www.sallymelvilleknits.com, and click on "Books."

Tiny Stocking

DESIGNED BY SALLY

I know there are lots of little sock patterns out there, but I couldn't do a Christmas chapter without offering one. And I found this to be the perfect number of stitches to beautifully highlight self-patterning sock yarns.

SKILL LEVEL
Intermediate

SIZE
All measurements are approximate.
> Height of leg 3" (7.5cm)
> Width 1¼" (3cm)

MATERIALS
> 20yd (18m) sock yarn, **1** superfine
> One set of 5 dpns, size 1 (2.25mm)
> One size E-4 (3.5mm) crochet hook (or size close to this)

GAUGE
Gauge does not matter.

Sock

LEG
Long-tail cast on 20 stitches.
Divide stitches evenly onto 4 dpns—5 stitches on each needle.
Join to work in the round, being careful not to twist cast-on edge.
Work in stockinette stitch until piece measures approximately 2½" (6.5 cm) OR you come to an appropriate change in the yarn's color pattern.

HEEL
Work back and forth over the heel.
RS Rows *Slip 1 purlwise, k1; repeat from * to 10 stitches on one needle. Turn.
Always slip 1 purlwise and with yarn to WS.
For all following rows, this will be written as "sl 1."
WS Rows Sl 1, p9.
RS Rows *Sl 1, k1; repeat from * 4 times more.
Repeat these 2 rows 4 times more, then repeat WS row once more.
Next Row (RS) Sl 1, k5, skp. Turn.
Next Row (WS) Sl 1, p2, p2tog. Turn.
Next Row (RS) Sl 1, k2, skp. Turn.
Repeat the last 2 rows once more, then repeat WS row once more—4 stitches.

INSTEP
Resume working in rounds.
Next Round Onto needle 1, k4 (from heel), then pick up and knit 6 stitches along slip-stitch edge of heel flap; onto needle 2, k5; onto needle 3, k5; onto needle 4, pick up and knit 6 stitches along remaining slip-stitch edge of heel flap, then k2 (from needle 1)—8 stitches on needles 1 and 4; 5 stitches on needles 2 and 3.
Rounds now begin at the center of sole.
Decrease Round Knit to last 2 stitches of needle 1, k2tog; knit to beginning of needle 4, skp, knit to end of needle 4.
Work 2 rounds even.
Repeat last 3 rounds twice more—5 stitches on each needle.

FOOT
Continue to work in rounds over 20 stitches until foot measures 1½" (3.8cm) past heel. End after working needle 1.
Rounds now begin at corner of instep.

TOE
Decrease Round Over first 3 stitches of needles 1 and 3, k1, skp,; over last 3 stitches of needles 2 and 4, k2tog, k1.
Work 1 round even.
Repeat the last 2 rounds once, then repeat decrease round once more—2 stitches on each needle.
Graft 4 stitches of needles 2 and 3 to 4 stitches of needles 1 and 4.

✳ TECHNIQUE ✳
If you don't know how to graft, you can just pull cut yarn through the remaining 8 stitches.

FINISHING
Cut 2yd (1.8m) length of yarn; fold in half.
Insert crochet hook through top-center back edge of sock, and draw the fold of the doubled yarn through the sock—to form loop onto crochet hook.
With doubled yarn, crochet 6" (15cm) chain.
Draw remaining yarn through last loop.
Sew tails to stocking to finish hanger.

8-Sided Tree

DESIGNED BY SALLY

I originally made this tree as a single, flat piece. (And you could do this by only making the first piece. If you are a novice knitter—or if you want to slip this ornament into a Christmas card— that might be a good choice.) But adding the second and third pieces was fun and not difficult.

SKILL LEVEL
Easy

SIZE
All measurements are approximate.
> Height (before felting) 4½" (11.5cm)
> Width (before felting) 3½" (9cm)
> Height (after felting) 4" (10cm)
> Width (after felting) 3" (7.5cm)

MATERIALS
> 24yd (22m) / 1 skein Cascade 220 (100% Peruvian highland merino wool, each 3.5oz [100g] and 220yd [198m]), in color 9425 (dark green), **4** medium
> One size 5 (3.75mm) circular needle, any length
> 74–90 beads with large holes
> 2 star buttons
> *Optional* 12" (30cm) wire, 26-gauge, green (to stabilize base)

GAUGE
Gauge does not matter.

Tree

FIRST PIECE
Thread half of beads onto yarn.
Long-tail cast on 18 stitches.

✽ TECHNIQUE ✽

Through the following rows of this piece, use all the threaded beads by bringing them up, one at a time, so they sit between stitches. Add beads randomly on both sides of work, so that the ornament is reversible.

All Rows Except Decrease Rows Wyif slip 1 purlwise, knit to end.
For all following directions, wyif slip 1 purlwise will be written as "sl 1."
*Decrease Row** Sl 1, skp, knit to last 3 stitches, k2tog.
Work 5 rows even.
Repeat from * until 4 stitches remain.
Next Row Skp, k2tog.
Work 1 row even.
K2tog.
Cut yarn, and draw through loop.

SECOND PIECE
Thread half of remaining beads onto yarn.
Turn first piece 90 degrees so that cast-on edge is at side.
*Find the "bump" that sits between 9th and 10th stitches of the first row.
Beginning at cast-on row, slip needle through this same bump up length of First Piece—24 bumps on needle.
Slip work so beginning of row is at cast-on edge, and knit 1 row.
Through the following rows of this piece, work threaded beads into the piece as First Piece.
Next (WS) Rows Sl 1, knit to end.
First Short Row Sl 1, knit to last 3 stitches. Turn.
Next (WS) Row Sl 1, knit to end.
Next Short Row Sl 1, knit to 3 stitches left behind. Turn.
Repeat the last 2 rows, leaving 3 more stitches un-worked each time.
Last Short Row Sl 1, k2. Turn.
Last (WS) Row Sl 1, k2.
Bind off 24 all stitches.
Cut yarn, and draw through loop.

THIRD PIECE

Thread remaining beads onto yarn.

Turn tree over to opposite side of First Piece.

Work as Second Piece from * to end.

If you run out of beads, thread more onto end of yarn.

FINISHING

Sew in all tails.

✳ TECHNIQUE ✳

Always sew in tails before felting your piece.

Otherwise, they may become matted messes.

Felt by washing ornament in hot water with cold rinse.

This will make it stiffer but not much smaller.

Dry in hot dryer.

Cut 2 pieces of yarn, 8″ (20.5cm) long. Thread them onto a tapestry needle, and draw both through the top of the tree, leaving 4″ (10cm) at each side.

Thread one star button onto both tails on one side, then thread the second star button onto both tails on the other side.

Tie a tight square knot with all tails to secure the stars to the top of the tree.

Tie an overhand knot towards the ends of the tails to make a 2″ (5cm) loop from which to hang the ornament: trim tails.

Optional To stabilize the bases, thread one 6″ (15cm) piece of wire across one base then a second 6″ (15cm) piece across the second. Bend the wires back at the ends to secure them.

North Star

DESIGNED BY SALLY

While it is not difficult, this is the most complex-looking, the most delicate, and the most traditional of the ornaments offered. I love its sweetness. But it does require a linen yarn, or something equally stiff—which is then further stiffened with spray starch.

SKILL LEVEL
Intermediate

SIZE
All measurements are approximate.
> Width 4" (10cm)
> Height 5" (12.5cm)

MATERIALS
> 10yd (9m) / 1 skein Louet Euroflax Sport Weight Linen (100% linen, each approximately 3½ oz [100g] and 270yd [243m]), in color 70 (white) or 30 (cream), (2) fine

Doubled lace-weight linen will achieve the same results.
> One size 3 (3.25mm) circular needle, any length
> One size B-1 (2.25mm) crochet hook (or size close to this)
> Spray starch
> *Optional* 24" (61cm) wired ribbon, ½–¾" (13mm–2cm) wide, any color

GAUGE
Gauge does not matter.

Star

BASE RING
Make slip knot, place on crochet hook.

Chain 16.

Draw yarn through first chain and through loop on hook to form circle.

Slip loop from crochet hook onto knitting needle: this becomes the right needle.

FIRST POINT
Row 1 (RS) With 1 stitch on right needle, *yo, pick up and k1 in next chain stitch of ring; repeat from * once—5 stitches. Turn.

Row 2 Wyif slip 1 p-wise, *kf&b into next yo, k1; repeat from * once—7 stitches.

Always slip wyif and p-wise. Further directions will read "sl 1."

Rows 3–6 Sl 1, knit to end.

Row 7 Sl 1, k1, sk2p, k2—5 stitches.

Rows 8–12 As Rows 3 to 6.

Row 13 Sl 1, sk2p, k1—3 stitches.

Rows 14–16 As Rows 3 to 6.

Row 17 Sk2p. Slip remaining stitch onto left needle. Kf&b&f (into this next stitch)—3 stitches.

You are forming a bobble at the end of the point.

Rows 18–20 Knit.

Row 21 Sk2p.

Leaving a 12" (30.5cm) tail, cut yarn and draw through last stitch.

Thread tail onto tapestry needle. Take needle through base of bobble just formed (to fold bobble over), and then wind yarn around base of bobble (to secure it). Make loop (to serve as hanger) with remaining yarn and before sewing in the tail.

SECOND–FIFTH POINTS
Row 1 With RS facing, pick up and knit 1 in next chain on ring, *yo, pick up and k1 in next chain on ring; repeat from * once—5 stitches.

Work as First Point from Row 2 to end, leaving only a 4" (10cm) tail.

Thread tail onto tapestry needle, and secure bobble as First Point.

FINISHING
Sew in all tails.

Lay star on wax paper, and spray both sides with spray starch.

With star still on wax paper, and with iron on cotton setting, iron it carefully.

Be careful not to let the star stick to the iron and burn.

Leave on paper to dry.

RIBBON (OPTIONAL)
Make a bow in center of ribbon, pulling very tight.

Turn bow over (to WS), and then turn 90 degrees.

Make a second bow over the first, pulling tight: 4 bow loops are formed.

Place bow on RS, over hole at center of star; take tails through hole (to hold the bow in place).

Trim tails of ribbon to suit.

Nordic Stocking

DESIGNED BY SALLY

How I wish I had made this stocking years ago for my own children who suffered through ugly, unimaginative, store-bought stockings. Those pieces were a family joke—and my personal shame—when shown to holiday visitors. Surely I will do better for my grandchildren? *These* will be lovely!

SKILL LEVEL
Experienced

SIZE
All measurements are approximate and after felting.
> Height (from top of cuff to center of heel) 16"
  (40.5cm)
> Circumference 15" (38cm)

MATERIALS
> Dale of Norway Heilo (100% wool, each ball approximately 1¾oz [50g] and 110yd [100m]), (2) fine, in the following amounts and colors:
> 200yd (180m) / 2 balls, in color 0090 (black) MC
> 120yd (112m) / 2 balls, in color 2931 (natural) C1
> 20yd (18m) / 1 ball, in color 4137 (red) C2
> 80yd (72m) / 1 ball, in color 9155 (olive green) C3
> Two size 5 (3.75mm) circular needles, 20–24"
  (51–61cm)
> 2 stitch markers
> One set of 5 dpns, size 5 (3.75mm)
> One size E-4 (3.5mm) crochet hook (or size close to this)

GAUGE
> Approximately 22 stitches and 24 rows = 4" (10cm) in stockinette stitch, before felting
> Approximately 24 stitches and 24 rows = 4" (10cm) in stockinette stitch, after felting
Gauge does not matter.

PATTERN NOTE
The colors indicated above are for the stocking shown to the right in the photo. For the alternative colorway (shown to the left in the photo), make the cuff as indicated, but use a clear green (color 7562) as MC for the stocking, a brighter white (color 0017) as C1 for the stocking, and black for the heel and toe. You will use the same number of balls of yarn.

Stocking

CUFF
Make a slip knot with both MC and C1 together.
Onto circular needle, long-tail cast on 96 stitches (not including slip knot) as follows: hold MC in front and C1

INSPIRATION

I designed this traditional Christmas stocking after my children had grown and because of a trip to the North Atlantic. In honor of the wonderful countries I visited, one chart is Norwegian, one is Icelandic, one is Danish, and one is Faroese.

in back. After casting on, remove slip knot.
*The stitches on needle will be C1: the lower edge of
cast-on will be MC.*
Form a circle, being careful not to twist cast-on edge.
Place marker to denote beginning of rounds.

※ TECHNIQUE ※

The following twisted braid demands that you are
constantly twisting and changing the colors. It is easier
to do this if you let the yarn hang, not wrapping it
through your fingers as you might normally do to knit.

In round 1, the yarns will twist—because one color is
always pulled into working over the alternate color.
Do not attempt to untwist them: do comb them apart
when needed to finish the round.

In round 2, the yarns will untwist automatically.

Braid Round 1 With both yarns in front, p1 in MC,
drop MC to front, *p1 in C1 (so C1 crosses above
MC), drop C1 to front, p1 in MC (so MC crosses
above C1), drop MC to front; repeat from * last stitch,
p1 in C1.
Braid Round 2 P1 in MC, lift MC, *p1 in C1 (so C1 crosses
under MC, then let MC fall), lift C1, p1 in MC (so it
crosses under C1, then let C1 fall); repeat from * to last
stitch, p1 in C1.
Cut C1.
Next 2 Rounds Knit in MC.
Rounds 1–8 Beginning with row 1, work heart chart in
MC and C2.
Cut C2.
Rounds 9–12 Beginning with row 9, work heart chart in
MC and C3.
Cut C3.
Next 2 Rounds Knit in MC.
Next Round Knit in C1.
Next 2 Rounds Repeat braid rounds 1 and 2 with MC
and C1.
Cut C1.

LEG
With MC, knit 1 round.
Next (Decrease) Round With MC, [k8, k2tog] 9 times,
end k6—87 stitches.
Continue to knit in MC and in rounds to ¼" (6mm)
short of cuff depth from its natural fold line.
Turn (so work is inside-out).
Knit in MC and in rounds to 1 round short of cuff depth.
Next Round K68, ending 19 stitches before marker.

Nordic Stocking

Place a new marker here, to indicate beginning of rounds; remove old marker when you encounter it.
Following Rounds With MC and C1, and beginning with row 1, work small box chart over 38 stitches (working from A to B 4 times, then working from B to C once); k1 in MC, k1 in C1, k1 in MC; work nordic star chart over 43 sts (working from D to E once); k1 in MC, k1 in C1, k1 in MC.

Continue to work in rounds and from charts until leg beyond the turned-over cuff measures 10" (25.5cm). End after working row 2, 6, 10, or 14 of small box chart, then continue with round over nordic star chart to 1 stitch before marker.
Note on what round you ended the nordic star chart.

HEEL

Onto 2 dpns, work back and forth over heel stitches as follows.
Remove marker when you encounter it.
Row 1 (RS) *With MC, slip 1 p-wise, k1, repeat from * to 40 stitches. Turn.
Always slip 1 p-wise and with yarn to WS. All following directions will read "sl 1."
Row 2 With MC, sl 1, p39. (Do not cut MC.)
Join C3. With C3 (instead of MC), repeat last 2 rows 18 times more—19 slip stitches up each side of Heel. End after working row 2.
Next Row Sl 1, k28, skp—9 stitches on left needle. Turn.
WS Rows Sl 1, p18, p2tog. Turn.
RS Rows Sl 1, k18, skp. Turn.
Repeat last 2 rows until only 20 stitches remain on dpn. End after working a WS row.
Cut C3.

INSTEP

Onto a second circular needle, with MC and RS facing, and beginning a lower right corner of heel, pick up

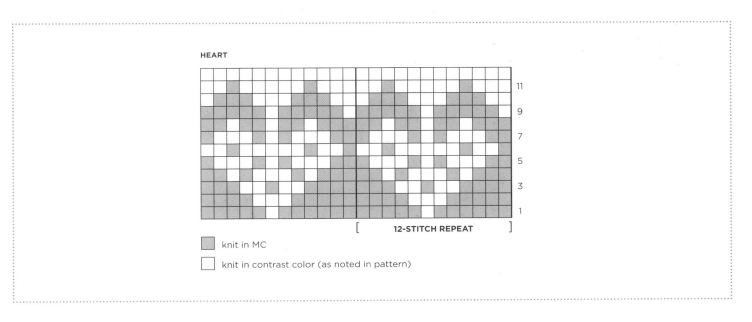

HEART

[**12-STITCH REPEAT**]

knit in MC

knit in contrast color (as noted in pattern)

and knit 20 stitches along slip-stitch edge; k9, k2tog, k9 along stitches of heel; pick up and knit 20 stitches along second slip-stitch edge of heel—59 stitches around heel, between C1s.

Place marker for beginning of round.

Cut C1 from other side of work and re-join here.

Continue onto original circular needle as follows.

Decrease Round K1 in C1, k1 in MC; work appropriate row of nordic star chart over 43 stitches; k1 in MC, k1 in C1; skp then k2 in MC, work row 1 of open box chart (by repeating from F to G until 7 stitches before marker), work from G to end of open box chart, end with k2 then k2tog in MC.

Next Round K1 in C1, k1 in MC; work nordic star chart over 43 stitches; k1 in MC, k1 in C1, k1 in MC; work open box chart to stitch before marker; k1 in MC.

Continue in patterns as established while repeating last 2 rounds—decreasing 2 stitches every other round (at both sides of open box pattern)—until 1 MC stitch on both sides plus 39 stitches remain in open box chart—88 stitches in stocking.

✷ TECHNIQUE ✷

Always work decreases in MC; do not work C1 stitch of open box chart if it will be disrupted by decreases.

FOOT

Continue in rounds and charts as established until foot measures approximately 5½" (14cm) beyond heel and to a good place in the color pattern to stop both the nordic star and open box patterns.

If you have already finished the open box pattern at a good place, you may work its final round in MC only.

End at marker. Remove marker, then k1 in C1.

Cut MC and C1.

TOE

Use C3 for toe.

Transfer knitting onto dpns as you work the next round.

Next Round Onto needle 1, k22; onto needle 2, k23; onto needle 3, k21; onto needle 4, k22.

Decrease Round Over first 3 stitches of needle 1, k1,

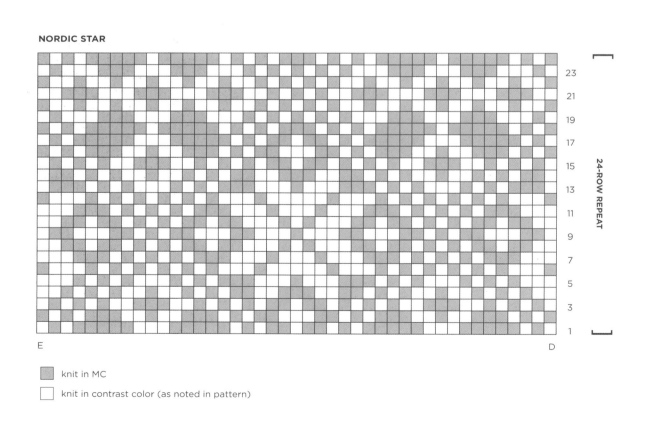

NORDIC STAR

23
21
19
17
15
13
11
9
7
5
3
1

24-ROW REPEAT

E

D

☐ knit in MC

☐ knit in contrast color (as noted in pattern)

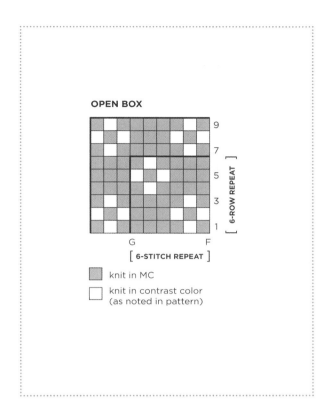

OPEN BOX

9
7
[6-ROW REPEAT]
5
3
1

G   F

[6-STITCH REPEAT]

■ knit in MC

□ knit in contrast color
(as noted in pattern)

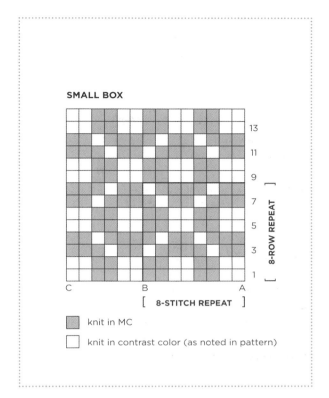

SMALL BOX

13
11
9
[8-ROW REPEAT]
7
5
3
1

C   B   A

[8-STITCH REPEAT]

■ knit in MC

□ knit in contrast color (as noted in pattern)

skp; over last 3 stitches of needle 2, k2tog, k1—21 on needles 1 and 3; 22 stitches on needles 2 and 4.
Work 1 round even.

Decrease Round Over first 3 stitches of needles 1 and 3, k1, skp; over last 3 stitches of needles 2 and 4, k2tog, k1.
Work 1 round even.
Repeat the last 2 rounds 11 times more—9, 10, 9, 10 stitches.
Place stitches onto 2 needles, and graft toe stitches together.

FINISHING

HANGER
Tack cuff down in 4 places.
With MC and crochet hook, crochet 3" (7.5cm) chain.
Fold chain in half and sew ends securely through all layers of cuff and to WS at center back, to form a hanger.

Sew in all tails before felting.
Felt by washing as directed in wool-wash solution; toss in dryer with towels on low heat for 5 minutes; turn dryer to air fluff, and remove when desired.

✳ TECHNIQUE ✳

I am told that weavers do this minimal felting to their fabrics, to make them "bloom." It does make the stitches "fatter" without creating a dense fabric that lacks stitch definition. I do it a lot with my wools (see the Skating Coat, page 131). But do experiment on a swatch, and *do not walk away from your dryer!*

This method of felting will plump the fabric nicely without the hard shrinkage that happens with soap, change of water temperature, and agitation.

Log Cabin Christmas Tree Skirt

DESIGNED BY SALLY

If doing a chapter dedicated to Christmas, the "big item" would have to be a tree skirt. And while I was originally not sure if I wanted one, I asked my friends . . . only to find that they love theirs. So I thought about it some more . . . played with yarn . . . chose colors . . . and created something I treasure.

SKILL LEVEL

Intermediate

SIZE

Finished radius (not including center circle or points) 23" (58.5cm)

Finished diameter (including center circle and points) 68" (172.5cm)

Finished circumference 215" (546cm)

MATERIALS

> Paton's Classic Wool (100% wool, each approximately 3½ oz [100g]), and 223yd [205m], (4) medium, in the following amounts and colors:
> 3330yd (3000m) / 15 balls, in color 220 (dark green) MC
> 400yd (360m) / 2 balls each, in colors 77208 (turquoise) C5, 240 (chartreuse) C6
> 300yd (270m) / 2 balls each, in colors 208 (dark red) C2, 77307 (eggplant) C3, 212 (purple) C4
> 200yd (180m) / 1 ball, in color 207 (red) C1
> One circular needle, size 10¾ (7mm), 24–32" (60–80cm), or size needed to obtain gauge
> One spare circular needle, 2–4 sizes smaller than main needle, 32" (81cm) (to use as holder)
> One size 10-J (6mm) crochet hook (or size close to this)

GAUGE

13 stitches and 26 rows = 4" (10cm) in double garter ridge and with doubled yarn

INSPIRATION

After much thought, and figuring, and swatching, my inspiration was my mother-in-law's favorite quilt block—the Log Cabin. It seemed the perfect image to honor the tree that sits at the center of the family's home at Christmas. The next puzzle to solve was how to make the wedge shape. I was fascinated through the figuring and the knitting, and I am thrilled with the result.

✳ FLATTER & FIT ✳

To make the piece larger, use larger needles. (And if you wash the garment in a wool-wash solution, it will likely stretch to 10 percent larger.)

STITCH PATTERN
Double Garter Ridge
Rows 1 and 2 Knit.
Rows 3 and 4 Purl.

Skirt

LOG CABIN SQUARE PANELS (MAKE 12)
PIECE 1
Use doubled yarn throughout.

✳ TECHNIQUE ✳

The most efficient way to use yarn doubled is to work from the inside plus the outside of the same ball.

With C1, long-tail cast on 8 stitches.
Beginning with row 2, work double garter ridge for 15 more rows (4 double garter ridges). End after working row 4.
Cut C1.

✳ TECHNIQUE ✳

Work in all tails as you go and as follows: for the initial tail, knit it in or weave it over its first row; for the final tail, weave it over the first row of the piece that is added above that piece. (See Glossary, page 167.) Do not trim woven tails to less than ¾" (2cm).

PIECE 2
With C2, C3, or C4.
*Work to 8 rows in double garter ridge.
End Piece Cut yarn, put stitches onto spare needle, turn work 90 degrees to right.

PIECE 3
With C2, C3, or C4, pick up and knit along 12 purl bumps at edge at edge of Pieces 2 and 1.

✳ TECHNIQUE ✳

Choose colors by distributing them evenly but not using it in the following Piece or on top of itself, or beside itself.

Always pick up and knit (see Glossary, page 167) into purl bumps close to—but not right at—the edge of the piece.

Work as * to end of Piece 2.

PIECE 4

With C5, C6, or MC, pick up and knit 4 stitches along purl bumps at edge of Piece 3 and 8 stitches along cast-on row—12 stitches.

Work as * to end of Piece 2.

PIECE 5

With C5, C6, or MC, pick up and knit 16 stitches along purl bumps at edges of Pieces 4, 1, and 2.

Work as * to end of Piece 2.

The spare needle will now completely encircle the piece.

PIECE 6

With C2, C3, or C4, pick up and knit 4 stitches along purl bumps at edge of Piece 5, 8 stitches from spare needle, and 4 stitches along purl bumps of Piece 3—16 stitches.

Work as * to end of Piece 2.

PIECE 7

With C2, C3, or C4, pick up and knit 4 stitches along purl bumps at edge of Piece 6, 12 stitches from spare

needle, and 4 stitches along purl bumps at edge of Piece 4—20 stitches.

Work as * to end of Piece 2.

PIECE 8

With C5, C6, or MC, pick up and knit 4 stitches along purl bumps at edge of Piece 7, 12 stitches from spare needle, and 4 stitches along purl bumps at edge of Piece 5—20 stitches.

Work as * to end of Piece 2.

PIECE 9

With C5, C6, or MC, pick up and knit 4 stitches along purl bumps at edge of Piece 8, 16 stitches from spare needle, and 4 stitches along purl bumps at edge of Piece 6—24 stitches.

Work as * to end of Piece 2.

PIECE 10

With C2, C3, or C4, pick up and knit 4 stitches along purl bumps at edge of Piece 9, 16 stitches from spare needle, and 4 stitches along purl bumps at edge of

Log Cabin Christmas Tree Skirt

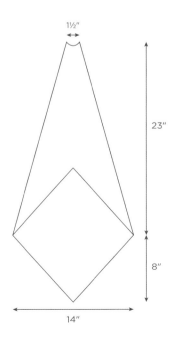

1½"

23"

8"

14"

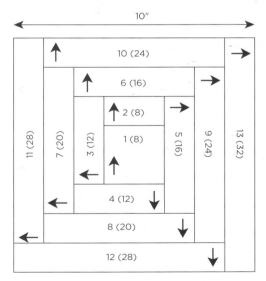

10"

10 (24)
6 (16)
2 (8)
11 (28)
7 (20)
3 (12)
1 (8)
5 (16)
9 (24)
13 (32)
4 (12)
8 (20)
12 (28)

ARROW INDICATES DIRECTION OF KNITTING

> First number is the number of the piece.
> Number in parentheses is the number of stitches.

Piece 7—24 stitches.

Work as * to end of Piece 2.

PIECE 11

With C2, C3, or C4, pick up and knit 4 stitches along purl bumps at edge of Piece 10, 20 stitches from spare needle, and 4 stitches along purl bumps at edge of Piece 8—28 stitches.

Work as * to end of Piece 2.

PIECE 12

With C5 or C6, pick up and knit 4 stitches along purl bumps at edge of Piece 11, 20 stitches from spare needle, and 4 stitches along purl bumps at edge of Piece 9—28 stitches.

Do not use MC for sections 12 or 13.

Work as * to end of Piece 2.

PIECE 13

With C5 or C6, pick up and knit 4 stitches along purl bumps at edge of Piece 12, 24 stitches from spare needle, and 4 stitches along purl bumps at edge of Piece 10—32 stitches.

Work to 8 rows of double garter ridge. Cut yarn.

MAIN COLOR EDGING

Slip needle back to beginning of piece 12, ready to work a RS row.

With MC, knit 28 stitches from spare needle, then pick up and knit 4 stitches along purl bumps at edge of Piece 13—32 stitches.

*Beginning with a WS row, knit 1 row, purl 1 row, knit 1 row, then bind off purlwise. Do not cut yarn, but draw ball of yarn through final stitch.

Turn work 90 degrees to right.*

Pick up and knit 2 stitches along purl bumps of edging just knit, then knit 32 stitches of piece 13.
Work as from * to * above.

MAIN COLOR UPPER PIECE

Pick up and knit as follows:
- 2 stitches along purl bumps of MC edging just knit
- 4 stitches along purl bumps at edge of Piece 13
- 24 stitches from spare needle
- 4 stitches from purl bumps at edge of Piece 11—34 stitches to corner
- 1 stitch at corner
- Place marker (to denote center stitch)
- 28 stitches from spare needle
- 4 stitches along purl bumps at edge of Piece 12
- 2 stitches along purl bumps of first MC edging—34 stitches from marker

—69 stitches on needle.

Beginning with row 2, work as follows.

Rows 1 and 5 K1, k2tog, knit to 2 stitches before marker, work lifted increase in next stitch, k1 (center stitch), work lifted increase in next stitch, knit to last 3 stitches, skp, k1.

Row 2 and 6 (WS) Wyif sl 1 p-wise, skp, knit to marker, wyif sl 1 p-wise, knit to last 3 stitches, k2tog, wyif sl 1 p-wise.

Row 3 and 7 K1, p2tog, purl to 2 stitches before marker, work lifted increase in next stitch, k1 (center stitch), work lifted increase in next stitch, purl to last 3 stitches, p2tog, k1.

Row 4 Sl 1 p-wise, p2tog, purl to marker, sl 1 p-wise, purl to last 3 stitches, p2tog, sl 1 p-wise.

Row 8 Sl 1 p-wise, purl to marker, sl 1 p-wise, purl to last stitch, sl 1 p-wise.

✱ TECHNIQUE ✱

For RS rows, increases balance decreases and produce the chevron pattern. For WS rows, decreases (every 3 of 4 WS rows) produce the pie-shape.

For rows 7 and 8, the number of stitches between slip stitches will be a multiple of 3.
Repeat last 8 rows until 9 stitches remain (3 stitches between slip stitches) after row 7.
Final Row (WS) Bind off purlwise.
Draw yarn through final stitch, leaving long tail for seaming.

INSPIRATION

When working through the design process for this piece, I didn't start with doubled yarn. But it soon became apparent that singled yarn would be a whole lot of knitting and would produce a light fabric that wouldn't hold shape once presents were piled onto it. Doubling the yarn solved both problems: a classic "two-fer!"

FINISHING

Sew seams between panels by taking outside edges of slip stitches into seam allowances.
Sew 11 seams between 12 panels, leaving 1 edge open.

TIES (MAKE 6)

Make ties along open edge—one pair at top, one pair at bottom, and one pair at center—as follows:
- Measure 2yd (1.8m) doubled lengths of MC
- Fold doubled yarn
- With crochet hook, draw doubled yarn at fold through spot along open edge, to form loop on hook
- Wrap 4 strands of yarn around crochet hook, and crochet a chain (of 4 strands) until very little of tails remain
- Draw remaining tails through loop on hook, and cut to 1" (2.5cm).

Tie bows to hold open edges together.

Mini Einstein Coat

DESIGNED BY SALLY

This piece is a miniature version of the coat that appears in my learn-to-knit book, *The Knit Stitch*. I've been told by countless knitters how beloved it is and how many versions have been made, so I thought, "Why not make a little one for the tree!"

SKILL LEVEL
Beginner

SIZE
All measurements are approximate.
> Height 3½" (9cm)
> Width 5½" (14cm)

MATERIALS
> 12–15yd (11–14m) yarn, any color, 3 or 4 light or medium
> One pair size 6-7 (4–4.5mm) needles
> One size G-6 (4mm) crochet hook
> 1 large (or 2 small) buttons
> 12" (30.5cm) wire, 18-gauge
> *Optional* 12" (30.5cm) ribbon, any width and color

GAUGE
Approximately 16 stitches and 32 rows = 4" (10cm), in stitch pattern
Gauge does not matter.

STITCH PATTERN
All Rows Wyif slip 1 purlwise, knit to end.

Coat

LOWER BODY PIECE
Crochet cast on 10 stitches.

✳ TECHNIQUE ✳
The crochet cast-on mimics the bind-off (see Glossary, page 167). But you may substitute with the knitted cast-on.

Work stitch pattern to 40 rows (20 ridges). End after working a WS row.
Bind off.

UPPER RIGHT FRONT
With RS facing and beginning at cast-on edge, pick up and knit 1 stitch in cast-on edge and 6 stitches in back of next 6 slip stitches along side edge of Lower Body Piece. Turn.
Work stitch pattern over 7 stitches for 9 more rows (5 ridges). End after working a WS row.
Bind off.

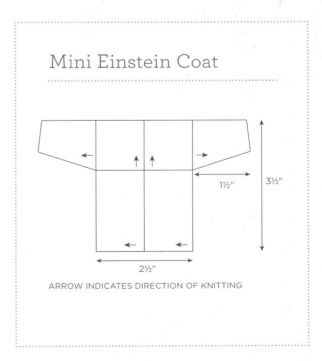

Mini Einstein Coat

1½"
3½"
2½"

ARROW INDICATES DIRECTION OF KNITTING

UPPER BACK

Beginning in same slip stitch as last picked-up stitch of Right Front, pick up and knit 10 stitches in back of next 10 slip stitches. Turn.

Work stitch pattern over 10 stitches for 9 more rows (5 ridges). End after working a WS row.

Bind off.

UPPER LEFT FRONT

Beginning in same slip stitch as last picked-up stitch of the Back, pick up and knit 6 stitches in back of next 6 slip stitches and then 1 stitch in bound-off edge.

Work stitch pattern over 7 stitches for 9 more rows (5 ridges). End after working a WS row.

Bind off.

RIGHT SLEEVE

Beginning at bound-off edge of Right Front, pick up and knit 1 stitch in bound-off edge and then 5 stitches in back of slip stitches down side edge to underarm—6 stitches.

Continue in same manner up side edge of Back, ending in bound-off edge—12 stitches.

*Work stitch pattern for 3 rows.

Decrease Row (RS) Work stitch pattern to 4 stitches on right needle, k2tog, skp, knit to end—10 stitches.

Work stitch pattern for 3 rows.

Decrease Row (RS) Work stitch pattern to 3 stitches on right needle, k2tog, skp, knit to end—8 stitches.

Work stitch pattern for 3 rows.

Bind off.

LEFT SLEEVE

Beginning in bound-off edge of Back and ending in bound-off edge of Left Front, pick up and knit as Right Sleeve.

Continue as Right Sleeve from * to end.

FINISHING

Sew Sleeve and shoulder seams to 4 stitches open at Front necks.

✳ TECHNIQUE ✳

I like to take half of a slip stitch or bound-off edge stitch from each side into the seam allowance.

Sew 1–2 buttons to close Fronts.

Bend the wire to form a coat hanger, approximately 4″ (10cm) wide and 2″ (5cm) tall. Slip the coat hanger into the piece.

Optional (Not Shown) With ribbon, tie a bow around the hanger—to sit at the neck.

Appendix

Glossary

3-needle bind-off
Hold two needles with stitches in left hand and with right sides together: with a third needle, work 2 stitches together (1 from each left-hand needle) while binding off as usual.

back
The side of the knitting not closest to you

bind off
Work 2 stitches, pass first stitch over second, *work 1 stitch, pass previous stitch over stitch just worked; repeat from *. (Always bind off in pattern unless directed otherwise.)

blanket stitch
With a length of yarn on a tapestry needle, make a series of running loops along an edge, bringing working yarn through the loop before pulling taut.

C or CC
Color or Contrast Color

cable cast-on
Begin with 2 e-wrap stitches, *insert right needle behind leading stitch, draw through yarn (as if to knit a new stitch), but without removing old stitch from left needle, put new stitch onto left needle; repeat from *; after a few stitches are cast on, remove first e-wrap cast-on stitch.

cast on
Add a number of stitches to left needle. (If we think you should use a particular cast-on method, we will tell you so; otherwise, use your preferred method.)

cn
Cable needle

crochet cast-on
Put slip knot onto crochet hook and hold hook in right hand. Hold knitting needle in left hand; hold yarn in left hand and behind needle. Take hook over needle, and draw yarn through slip knot; *take yarn between hook and needle to return it to back of needle; take hook over needle, and draw yarn through loop on hook; repeat from *. When one fewer stitch is on needle than required, return yarn to behind needle, and put loop from hook onto needle.

crochet chain
Start with a slip knot, or loop, on crochet hook; *with hook, draw yarn through loop on hook—1 chain stitch formed; repeat from *.

double garter ridge
*Knit 2 rows, then purl 2 rows; repeat from *.

dpn
Double-pointed needle

duplicate stitch
A form of embroidery in which the embroidered yarn duplicates the knit stitch

e-wrap cast-on
With both tail and needle in left hand, *take right index finger around working yarn (over top then under), then insert needle through twisted loop on finger; repeat from *.

felt
To deliberately shrink (usually wool) with change of water temperature and/or agitation and/or soap.

front
The side of the knitting closest to you

garter (stitch)
Knit every row.

garter ridge
The ridge formed by two knit rows *or* a stitch pattern formed by two knit rows followed by two purl rows

graft
A method of sewing live stitches together that looks like a row of knitting

I-cord
This is usually done on double-pointed needles, but it can be done on a circular. Cast on stitches (usually 2 or 3). *Knit stitches from left needle onto right, without turning right needle, slide these stitches to beginning of needle, (This now becomes the left needle), repeat from *.

intarsia
Working with more than one color in a row, each with its own ball (or strand) of yarn, twisted at the color change (by taking the previous color over the next color)

k
Knit.

k2tog

Insert right needle knitwise into second and then first stitch on left needle, then knit both together—1 stitch decreased with a right-side, right-slanting decrease.

k3tog

Insert right needle into third, and second, and then first stitch on left needle, then knit them all together—2 stitches decreased with a right-side, right-slanting decrease.

kf&b

Knit into front and then back of next stitch—1 stitch increased, 2 stitches from 1.

kf&b&f

Knit into front, and then back, and then again into front of next stitch—2 stitches increased, 3 stitches from 1.

kf&b&f&b

Knit into front, and then back, and then again into front, and then again into back of next stitch—3 stitches increased, 4 stitches from 1.

knitwise (k-wise)

As if to knit

knitted cast-on

*Insert needle into leading stitch (or slip knot) on left needle, draw through yarn (as if to knit a new stitch), but, without removing old stitch from left needle, put new stitch onto left needle; repeat from *.

knitting in tails

Knit with the tail and the main yarn until ¾" (2cm) remains of the tail.

lifted increase

Work into stitch below *or* into right "leg" of stitch below next stitch on left needle (knitwise or purlwise, as indicated by stitch pattern), then work stitch on left needle (as indicated by stitch pattern—1 stitch increased.

long-tail cast-on

Have long tail over front of right needle and rest of yarn in back. Hold both strands of yarn in left hand, then spread yarn apart with left thumb and index finger. Take right needle under front of "thumb" yarn, over "finger" yarn, then draw "finger" yarn through space produced by "thumb" yarn. Pull both taut. (Pulling on the "thumb" yarn tightens the cast-on edge.)

M1 (make 1)

Lift thread that sits between stitches on right needle and left needle; knit into it so as to twist it.

MC

Main color

p

Purl.

p2tog

Insert right needle purlwise into first and then second stitch on left needle, then purl both together—1 stitch decreased with a right-side, right-slanting decrease.

pick up

From left to right, insert needle into bumps (usually garter) that sit on row edge of knitting. This becomes left needle.

pick up and knit

Insert right needle through an edge, one stitch from the edge *or* below cast-on or bound-off edge. (This takes 1 selvedge stitch *or* bound-off *or* cast-on edge into seam allowance.) To not get holes, insert needle so as to have 2 threads on needle. Draw through yarn to make a stitch—1 stitch picked up and knit.

pm

Place marker.

psso

Pass slip stitch over.

purlwise (p-wise)

As if to purl

reading charts

Read all charts from right to left on right-side rows and from left to right on wrong-side rows. If working in the round, read all charts from right to left. If repeat lines are indicated, repeat the stitches within these lines as many times as possible or as directed.

reverse stockinette (RSS)

Purl right-side rows; knit wrong-side rows.

rib

A repeated combination of knits and purls, usually presented as follows: 2x4 = 2 RS knits followed by 2 RS purls (Unless otherwise indicated, all RS knits are worked as purls on WS rows, and vice versa.)

right (left) front

The part of the garment worn on your right (left) front

round

Indicates a "row" of knitting worked in the round

row
A row of knitting worked back and forth

RS
Right side

seaming
Hold pieces with right sides facing. Taking 1 stitch from each edge *or* bound-off edge *or* cast-on edge into seam allowances, sew pieces together.

short row
Turn before the end of the row.

single crochet (sc)
Begin with loop on crochet hook. Insert hook through work, and wrap yarn around hook, then pull this loop through work (two loops now on hook); take hook over work, wrap yarn around hook, and draw this yarn through both loops on hook—1 single crochet made.

s2kp
Slip 2 stitches together and knitwise, knit 1 from left needle, pass both slip stitches over, together—2 stitches decreased with a right-side, non-slanting decrease.

skp
Slip 1 knitwise, knit 1 from left needle, pass slip stitch over—1 stitch decreased with a right-side, left-slanting decrease.

sk2p
Slip 1 knitwise, knit next 2 stitches together, pass slip stitch over—2 stitches decreased with a right-side, left-slanting decrease

slip (sl)
Slip next stitch from left needle onto right. We tell you if you should slip knitwise or purlwise. Also, if not told to do so, do not move the yarn.

slip knot
Hold tail in left hand. Wrap yarn behind fingers of left hand, then to back again; bring yarn through circle of yarn on left fingers to create loop; tighten as needed.

ssk
Slip next 2 stitches, one at a time and knitwise, from left needle onto right, insert left needle into front of these two stitches, and knit them together—1 stitch decreased with a right-side, left-slanting decrease.

stockinette stitch
Knit right-side rows; purl wrong-side rows.

twist
Usually in reference to a yo, this means to work the yo on the following row to "twist" it—done by working through the non-leading edge (i.e., the part of the stitch not sitting closest to the tip of the needle).

weaving in tails
*With the left hand, lift the tail; with the main yarn, work "under" the tail. Drop the tail; work the next stitch as usual. Repeat from *. (It does not matter if you work with the yarn in the right or left hand.)

working in the round
Working on double-pointed needles or on a circular needle, continue working from the left needle onto the right without turning the work.

wyib
With yarn in back of work (away from you)

wyif
With yarn in front of work (toward you)

WS
Wrong side

yo
On a knit row, bring yarn to front, then knit next stitch as usual—1 new stitch made. On a purl row, wrap yarn around right needle—1 new stitch made. On next row, never twist this stitch unless directed to do so.

Yarn Index

All of the projects in this book call for materials that are readily available at yarn or craft stores. The following list of suppliers will help you find all the materials you need to complete the projects in the book.

Sometimes a yarn's weight can straddle more than one weight category (as offered in the CYCA chart). Its label may only offer one category, whereas the pattern knits it to an alternative. In the patterns and in the list below, we have listed the yarn by weight according to how it is labeled. This will be most helpful if you make substitutions. But do make a gauge swatch to ensure accuracy.

Weight 0 (lace)
Curious Creek Fibers Meru (51% tussah silk, 49% merino, each approximately 1¾ oz [50g] and 495yd [450m]), in color yellow brick road, for My First Lace Scarf, page 48.

Goldschild or Londonderry Linen Thread nel 80/3 (100% linen, each approximately 390yd [350m]), in color 15 (ivory), for Lace Bookmarks, page 50.

Malabrigo Lace (100% baby merino, each approximately 1¾ oz [50g] and 470yd [425m]), in colors 19 (pollen), 72 (apricot), 17 (pink frost), 83 (water green), 37 (lettuce), 35 (frank ochre), for Blended Baby Blanket, page 10.

Weight 1 (superfine)
Diamond Luxury Collection Alpaca Prima (100% alpaca, each approximately 1¾ oz [50g] and 185yd [169m]), in color 2095 (red brick), for Center-Paneled Vest / Sweater, page 107.

Punta Yarns MeriSock Handpainted (95% merino wool, 5% nylon, each approximately 3½ oz [100g] and 463yd [417m]), in color HP72 (chartreuse and navy), for Center-Paneled Vest / Sweater, page 107.

Weight 2 (fine)
Dale of Norway Heilo (100% wool, each ball approximately 1¾ oz [50g] and 110yd [100m]), in colors 0090 (black), 2931 (natural), 4137 (red), 9155 (olive green), for Nordic Stocking, page 150.

Louet Euroflax Sport Weight Linen (100% linen, each approximately 3½ oz [100g] and 270yd [243m]), in color 70 (white) or 30 (cream), for North Star, page 148.

Rowan Classic Cashsoft 4ply (57% merino, 33% acrylic, 10% cashmere, each approximately 1¾ oz [50g] and 197yd [180m]), in color 433 (cream), for Baby Doll Dress, page 71, and in color 432 (brown), for Petticoat, page 77.

Weight 3 (light)
Berroco Touche (50% cotton, 50% rayon, each approximately 1¾ oz [50g] and 89yd [82m]), in color 7944 (pebble), for Heirloom Jumper, page 140.

Classic Elite Classic One Fifty (100% fine merino, each approximately 1¾ oz [50g] and 150yd [135m]), in colors 7238 (chestnut), 7206 (sand), 7214 (elfin green), for Argyle Watchband, page 44, and in colors 7203 (pewter) and 7281 (ember glow) for Arm Warmers, page 88.

Rowan Classic Cashsoft DK (57% extra fine merino, 33% acrylic, 10% cashmere, each approximately 1¾ oz [50g] and 142yd [130m]), in color 517 (donkey), for Andy's Polo, page 53.

Rowan Denim (100% cotton, each approximately 1¾ oz [50g] and 102yd [93m]), in color 225 (Nashville), for Groovy Pullover, page 79.

Sirdar Snuggly (55% nylon, 45% acrylic, each approximately 1¾ oz [50g] and 191yd [175m]), in colors 0312 (black) and 0251 (white), for Baby's First Doll, page 31.

Weight 4 (medium)
Brown Sheep Cotton Fleece (80% cotton, 20% merino wool, each approximately 3½ oz [100g] and 215yd [197m]), in colors 590 (lapis), 310 (wild orange), 005 (cavern), and 100 (cotton ball), for Kids' Sport Sweater, page 36.

Cascade 220 (100% Peruvian highland merino wool, each 3.5oz [100g] and 220yd [198m]), in color 9425 (dark green), for 8-Sided Tree, page 146.

Cascade Yarns Soft Spun (100% Peruvian highland wool, each approximately 3½ oz [100g] and 197yd [180m]), in color 2808 (natural), for Simple Felted Scarf, page 86.

Cleckheaton Country Naturals 8ply (85% wool, 10% acrylic, 5% viscose, each approximately 1¾ oz [50g] and 105yd [95m]), in color 1832 (gray), for Vested Hoodie, page 25.

Diamond Galway Highland Heather (100% wool, each approximately 3½ oz [100g] and 220yd [200m]), in colors 700 (ruddy heather), 638 (midnight blue), 701 (teal), 620 (claret), 687 (forest), 705 (moss), for Add-On Afghan, page 94.

Lana Grossa Maxi Tosca (55% wool, 45% acrylic, each approximately 1¾ oz [50g] and 102yd [92m]), in color 0068 (variegated), for Sean's Fingerless Gloves, page 119.

Louet MerLin (70% merino wool, 30% linen, each approximately 3½ oz [100g] and 156yd [140m]), in colors 18 (aqua) and 36 (linen grey) for Baby Overalls, page 20.

Mirasol Miski (100% baby llama, each approximately 1¾ oz [50g] and 82yd [75m]), in color 108 (copper), for Center-Paneled Vest / Sweater, page 107.

Nashua Cilantro (70% cotton, 30% polyester, each approximately 1¾ oz [50g] and 136yd [125m]), in color NCIL011 (delft blue), for The Cardigan Caddy Really Wanted, page 58, and in color NCIL022 (lavender gray), for The Sweater Sally Made Instead, page 64.

Patons Classic Wool (100% wool, each approximately 3½ oz [100g] and 223yd [205m]), in colors 205 (deep olive), 218 (peacock), 240 (leaf green), 212 (royal purple), for Glasses Case, page 46, and in colors 220 (dark green), 77208 (turquoise), 240 (chartreuse), 208 (dark red), 77307 (eggplant), 212 (purple), 207 (red), for Log Cabin Christmas Tree Skirt, page 156.

Punta Yarns Merisoft Space Dyed (100% merino, each approximately 3½ oz [100g] and 197yd [178m]), in color NM 1800 (chartreuse), for Center-Paneled Vest / Sweater, page 107.

Shelridge Farm Soft Touch W4 (100% wool, each approximately 3½ oz [100g] and 220yd [200m]), in color Autumn Orange, for Architectural Shawl, page 98.

Sublime Kid Mohair (60% kid mohair, 35% nylon, 5% extra fine merino, each approximately ⅞ oz [25g] and 122yd [112m]), in color 0069 (mouse), for Christmas Morning Sweater, page 113.

Tahki Yarns Donegal Tweed (100% pure new wool, each approximately 3½ oz [100g] and 183yd [167m]), in color 810 (fuchsia), for Cardilero, page 103.

Weight 5 (bulky)

Cascade Eco+ (100% wool, each approximately 8¾ oz [250g] and 478yd [437m]), in color 8511 (dark red), for Skating Coat, page 122.

Jil Eaton Minnow Merino (100% extra fine merino, each approximately 1¾ oz [50g] and 77yd [70m]), in color 4750 (yellow), for Ear Flap Baby Hat, page 180.

Misti International Alpaca Chunky (100% baby alpaca, each approximately 3½ oz [100g] and 110yd [100m]), in color C815 (chartreuse mélange), for Hooded Scarf, page 92.

Noro Iro (75% wool, 25% silk, each approximately 3½ oz [100g] and 132yd [120m]), in color 30 (variegated) for Sean's Fingerless Gloves, page 119.

Plymouth Alpaca Bouclee (90% alpaca / 10% nylon, each approximately 1¾ oz [50g] and 65yd [58m]), in color 14 (rust), for Vested Hoodie, page 25.

Weight 6 (super bulky)

Brown Sheep Company Burly Spun (100% wool, each approximately 4oz [114g] and 130yd [120m], in color 115 (oatmeal), for Peaked Cap, page 90.

CYCA Yarn Weights

0	1	2	3	4	5	6
LACE	SUPERFINE	FINE	LIGHT	MEDIUM	BULKY	SUPER BULKY

These weights are also known as the following.

lace	sock/fingering	sport	DK	worsted	chunky	bulky
fingering	baby	baby	light worsted	afghan	craft	roving/rug

This is the range of stitches they would achieve, worked in stockinette stitch and over 4" (10cm)

33–40	27–32	23–26	21–24	16–20	12–15	6–11

This is their (CYCA) recommended needle size, U.S. sizes.

000–1	1–3	3–5	5–7	7–9	9–11	11 and larger

This is their (CYCA) recommended needle size, metric sizes.

1.5–2.25mm	2.25–3.25mm	3.25–3.75mm	3.75–4.5mm	4.5–5.5mm	5.5–8mm	9–16mm

Resource List

Berroco Inc.
PO Box 367
14 Elmdale Rd.
Uxbridge, MA USA 01569
508-278-2527
www.berroco.com

Bookblanks
(for plastic bookmark sleeves)
www.bookblanks.com

Brown Sheep Company Inc.
100662 County Rd. 16
Mitchell, NE USA 69357
800-826-9136
www.brownsheep.com

Cascade Yarns Inc.
1224 Andover Park E.
Tukwilia, WA USA 98188
206-574-0440
www.cascadeyarns.com

Classic Elite Yarns
(For Classic Elite, Jil Eaton)
122 Western Ave.
Lowell, MA USA 01851-1434
800-444-5648
www.classiceliteyarns.com

Curious Creek Fibers Meru
3070 Palm St.
San Diego, CA USA 92104
619-280-3410
www.curiouscreek.com

Dale of Norway Inc.
4750 Shelburne Rd., Suite 20
Shelburne, VT USA 05482
802-383-0132
www.daleofnorway.com

Diamond Yarns
(for Diamond, Mirasol)
155 Martin Ross Ave., Unit 3
Toronto, ON Canada M3J 2L9
800-268-1896
www.diamondyarn.com

Knitting Fever Inc.
(for Mirasol, Noro, Sirdar, Sublime)
PO Box 336, 315 Bayview Ave.
Amityville, NY USA 11701
516-546-3600
www.knittingfever.com

Louet Sales
3425 Hands Rd.
Prescott, ON Canada K0E 1T0
613-925-4502
www.louet.com

Malabrigo Yarn
8424 NW 56th St., Suite #mvd
80496
Miami, FL USA 33116
786-866-6187
www.malabrigoyarn.com

Misti International
PO Box 2532
Glen Ellyn, IL USA 60138-2532
888-776-9276
www.mistialpaca.com

Muench Yarns, Inc.
(for Lana Grossa)
1323 Scott St.
Petaluma, CA USA 94954-1135
707-763-9377
www.muenchyarns.com

Plymouth Yarn Company Inc.
(for Plymouth, Cleckheaton)
500 Lafayette St.
Bristol, PA USA 19007
215-788-0459
www.plymouthyarn.com

Punta Yarns, Duchess Fibers
132 Church St., PO Box 221
Millbrook, NY USA 12545
845-677-4601
www.puntayarns.com

Shelridge Farm
PO Box 1345
Durham, ON Canada N0G 1R0
866-291-1566
www.shelridge.com

Skacel
PO Box 88110
Seattle, WA USA 98138-2110
800-255-1278
www.skacelknitting.com

Tahki • Stacy Charles Inc.
70-30 80th St., Bldg. #36
Glendale, NY USA 11385
800-338-9276
www.tahkistacycharles.com

Trillium Bobbin Lace
(for Goldschild or Londonderry
linen thread and plastic bookmark
sleeves)
32 McNaughton Ave.
Ottawa, ON Canada K1S 0J2
613-234-9791
www.trilliumlace.ca

Westminster Fibers
(for Nashua, Rowan)
165 Ledge St.
Nashua, NH USA 03060
800-445-9276
www.westminsterfibers.com

Sizing Charts

These are the standard measurements we have used to determine the sizes for this book. When determining which size you should knit, use these body measurements. We have then added the appropriate ease to the actual garment based on its style, or yarn, or stitch pattern.

WOMAN'S SIZES

SIZE	BUST	WAIST	HIPS
XS	28–30" (71–76cm)	20–22" (51–56cm)	30–32" (76–81cm)
S	32–34" (81–86cm)	24–26" (61–66cm)	34–36" (86–91cm)
M	36–38" (91–96.5cm)	28–30" (71–76cm)	38–40" (96.5–101.5cm)
L	40–42" (101.5–105.5cm)	32–34" (81–86cm)	42–44" (106.5–112cm)
1X	44–46" (112–117cm)	36–38" (91–96.5cm)	46–48" (117–122cm)
2X	48–50" (122–127cm)	40–42" (101.5–106.5cm)	50–52" (127–132cm)

MEN'S SIZES

SIZE	CHEST
S	34–36" (86–91cm)
M	38–40" (96.5–101.5cm)
L	42–44" (106.5–112cm)
1X	46–48" (117–122cm)
2X	50–52" (127–132cm)

BABY'S SIZES

SIZE	CHEST	HEAD CIRCUMFERENCE
newborn	15" (38cm)	14" (35.5cm)
3 mos	16" (40.5cm)	15" (38cm)
6 mos	17" (43cm)	16" (40.5cm)
12 mos	18" (45.5cm)	17" (43cm)

CHILDREN'S SIZES

SIZE	CHEST
2	21" (53.5cm)
4	23" (58.5cm)
6	25" (63.5cm)
8	26½" (67.5cm
10	28" (71cm)
12	30" (76cm)

Notes on Fit

We have made all women's garments for 5'4"–5'6" (163–168cm).

We have made all men's garments for 5'10"–6' (178–183cm).

For personalized length, look at a garment of the same style that is the right length, and work to this length. But if you aren't sure, here are some guidelines.

> **Ideal short length (for a short, unshaped sweater)** This garment usually lands at the fullest part of your belly (approximately 3" [7.5cm] below your navel).

> **Ideal mid-length (for a mid-length, shaped sweater)** This garment usually lands at your leg-break or the widest part of your hip, as revealed by the pants you'll wear with the garment (whichever is lower).

> **Ideal long length (for a long, shaped or unshaped sweater)** Wearing the pants you would wear with the garment, find the place down your leg before your hip width begins to show: this is where this garment usually lands.

> **Waist length** This is measured from the base of your neck, down your back, to your waist. It applies only to garments with waist shaping. Generally, you want to ensure that this shaping falls at the waist or above—never down on the hip.

> **Sleeve length** This is a tailoring term, and it refers to the length from center back, around the shoulder, down the bent arm, to the "wrist break." (The measurement is taken this way so this one number can apply to all styles of sweaters.) In garment measurements, it refers to half the width of the garment plus all the length of the sleeve.

> **Shoulder width** This is the measurement from armhole edge to armhole edge. Measure yourself from the sensitive spots on the tops of your shoulders, across your back. (Or measure a garment that fits well across the shoulders.)

> **Note** These measurements—how to aquire them, how to adjust for them, and what to wear with different lengths—are described in detail in *Mother-Daughter Knits,* in the Knit to Flatter and Fit chapter.

Needle and Hook Sizes

US	MM	HOOK
0	2	A
1	2.25	B
2	2.75	C
3	3.25	D
4	3.5	E
5	3.75	F
6	4	G
7	4.5	7

US	MM	HOOK
8	5	H
9	5.5	I
10	6	J
10 ½	6.5	K
10 ¾	7	-
11	8	L
13	9	M
15	10	N

Acknowledgments

First and foremost, thanks to Caddy for being so thoroughly and consistently brilliant, inventive, hard-working, and patient. I would wish all of you a similar joy in watching your child at work.

And second, thanks to Robert Cuerrier for creating Mockin'bird Hill Farm in Sault Ste Marie, Ontario, Canada. This place is, to me and for all seasons of the year, a paradise. (Robert has dedicated his life to re-creating the farm of a simpler time, and he works harder than most humans to offer an amazing environment for the edification and education of folks and families.) It was walking through this farm that this book was inspired.

And now my thanks go to . . .

the staff at Random House for patience through some tough decisions ✳ all yarn suppliers for faith, diligence, and understanding ✳ Kara Guild for conscientious editing ✳ Stasia Bania for knitting me whatever I needed as soon as I needed it ✳ my friends, especially the lovely Mel Biggs, for encouraging me in all things—and for persistence through the Christmas Tree Skirt ✳ Sean Riley for inspiring the Fingerless Gloves ✳ Dorinn Gould for knitting me a treasured lace bookmark and inspiring a similar project that I offer here ✳ my grandmother— "Honey" Poppy (Lyons-Bowes) Dure—whose color work inspired me so long ago with an afghan I still treasure ✳ Shannon Moore for hard and careful work when he would surely have preferred to spend his limited spare time doing something else ✳ Beverley Slopen, who has given me intelligent advice and patient support over the years and been my agent for my last two books, ✳ and to my children, and their partners, for producing two exquisite baby girls . . . in the same year! I now intend to spend some much-needed time off playing with those granddaughters!
                                                                    —SALLY

Huge thanks must go to . . .

Bridget and Christina whose humor, thoughtfulness, and generosity I couldn't live without ✳ my nephew Shannon whose ridiculous talent could keep him busy doing many things other than our schematics ✳ Jeremy and Eliana for giving exactly the kind of support I desperately needed; it has meant the world to me ✳ my mom who I will never be able to thank enough for her patience and wisdom, but I may be able to understand now that I have a daughter of my own ✳ and Andy for being such a beautiful husband and an even more beautiful father.
—CADDY

Index